Tartuffe by Molière

or The Hypocrite aka The Imposter

Tartuffe ou L'Imposteur

Jean-Baptiste Poquelin is better known to us by his stage name of Molière. He was born in Paris, to a prosperous well-to-do family on 15th January 1622.

In 1631, his father purchased from the court of Louis XIII the posts of "valet of the King's chamber and keeper of carpets and upholstery" which Molière assumed in 1641. The benefits included only three months' work per annum for which he was paid 300 livres and also provided a number of lucrative contracts.

However in June 1643, at 21, Molière abandoned this for his first love; a career on the stage. He partnered with the actress Madeleine Béjart, to found the Illustre Théâtre at a cost of 630 livres. Unfortunately despite their enthusiasm, effort and ambition the troupe went bankrupt in 1645.

Molière and Madeleine now began again and spent the next dozen years touring the provincial circuit. His journey back to the sacred land of Parisian theatres was slow but by 1658 he performed in front of the King at the Louvre.

From this point Molière both wrote and acted in a large number of productions that caused both outrage and applause. His many attacks on social conventions, the church, hypocrisy and other areas whilst also writing a large number of comedies, farces, tragicomedies, comédie-ballets are the stuff of legend.

'Tartuffe', 'The Misanthrope', 'The Miser' and 'The School for Wives' are but some of his classics.

His death was as dramatic as his life. Molière suffered from pulmonary tuberculosis. One evening he collapsed on stage in a fit of coughing and haemorrhaging while performing in the last play he'd written, in which, ironically, he was playing the hypochondriac Argan, in 'The Imaginary Invalid'.

Molière insisted on completing his performance.

Afterwards he collapsed again with another, larger haemorrhage and was taken home. Priests were sent for to administer the last rites. Two priests refused to visit. A third arrived too late. On 17th February 1673, Jean-Baptiste Poquelin, forever to be known as Molière, was pronounced dead in Paris. He was 51.

Index of Contents

DRAMATIS PERSONAE
Madame PERNELLE, mother of ORGON
ORGON, husband of ELMIRE
ELMIRE, wife of ORGON
DAMIS, son of ORGON
MARIANE, daughter of ORGON, in love with VALÈRE
CLEANTE, brother-in-law of ORGON
TARTUFFE, a hypocrite

DORINE, Mariane's maid
MR. LOYAL, a bailiff
A Police OFFICER
FLIPOTTE, Madame Pernelle's servant

TARTUFFE or, THE HYPOCRITE aka THE IMPOSTER [TARTUFFE OU L'IMPOSTEUR

ACT I

SCENE I

Madame PERNELLE and FLIPOTTE, her servant; **ELMIRE, MARIANE, CLEANTE, DAMIS, DORINE.**

Madame PERNELLE
Come, come, Flipotte, and let me get away.

ELMIRE
You hurry so, I hardly can attend you.

Madame PERNELLE
Then don't, my daughter-in law. Stay where you are.
I can dispense with your polite attentions.

ELMIRE
We're only paying what is due you, mother.
Why must you go away in such a hurry?

Madame PERNELLE
Because I can't endure your carryings-on,
And no one takes the slightest pains to please me.
I leave your house, I tell you, quite disgusted;
You do the opposite of my instructions;
You've no respect for anything; each one
Must have his say; it's perfect pandemonium.

DORINE
If ...

Madame PERNELLE
You're a servant wench, my girl, and much
Too full of gab, and too impertinent
And free with your advice on all occasions.

DAMIS
But ...

Madame PERNELLE
You're a fool, my boy f, o, o, l
Just spells your name. Let grandma tell you that
I've said a hundred times to my poor son,
Your father, that you'd never come to good
Or give him anything but plague and torment.

MARIANE
I think ...

Madame PERNELLE
O dearie me, his little sister!
You're all demureness, butter wouldn't melt
In your mouth, one would think to look at you.
Still waters, though, they say ... you know the proverb;
And I don't like your doings on the sly.

ELMIRE
But, mother ...

Madame PERNELLE
Daughter, by your leave, your conduct
In everything is altogether wrong;
You ought to set a good example for 'em;
Their dear departed mother did much better.
You are extravagant; and it offends me,
To see you always decked out like a princess.
A woman who would please her husband's eyes
Alone, wants no such wealth of fineries .

CLEANTE
But, madam, after all ...

Madame PERNELLE
Sir, as for you,
The lady's brother, I esteem you highly,
Love and respect you. But, sir, all the same,
If I were in my son's, her husband's, place,
I'd urgently entreat you not to come
Within our doors. You preach a way of living
That decent people cannot tolerate.
I'm rather frank with you; but that's my way
I don't mince matters, when I mean a thing.

DAMIS
Mr. Tartuffe, your friend, is mighty lucky ...

Madame PERNELLE

He is a holy man, and must be heeded;
I can't endure, with any show of patience,
To hear a scatterbrains like you attack him.

DAMIS

What! Shall I let a bigot criticaster
Come and usurp a tyrant's power here?
And shall we never dare amuse ourselves
Till this fine gentleman deigns to consent?

DORINE

If we must hark to him, and heed his maxims,
There's not a thing we do but what's a crime;
He censures everything, this zealous carper.

Madame PERNELLE

And all he censures is well censured, too.
He wants to guide you on the way to heaven;
My son should train you all to love him well.

DAMIS

No, madam, look you, nothing not my father
Nor anything can make me tolerate him.
I should belie my feelings not to say so.
His actions rouse my wrath at every turn;
And I foresee that there must come of it
An open rupture with this sneaking scoundrel.

DORINE

Besides, 'tis downright scandalous to see
This unknown upstart master of the house
This vagabond, who hadn't, when he came,
Shoes to his feet, or clothing worth six farthings,
And who so far forgets his place, as now
To censure everything, and rule the roost!

Madame PERNELLE

Eh! Mercy sakes alive! Things would go better
If all were governed by his pious orders.

DORINE

He passes for a saint in your opinion.
In fact, he's nothing but a hypocrite.

Madame PERNELLE

Just listen to her tongue!

DORINE

I wouldn't trust him,
Nor yet his Lawrence, without bonds and surety.

Madame PERNELLE
I don't know what the servant's character
May be; but I can guarantee the master
A holy man. You hate him and reject him
Because he tells home truths to all of you.
'Tis sin alone that moves his heart to anger,
And heaven's interest is his only motive.

DORINE
Of course. But why, especially of late,
Can he let nobody come near the house?
Is heaven offended at a civil call
That he should make so great a fuss about it?
I'll tell you, if you like, just what I think;

[Pointing to **ELMIRE**.

Upon my word, he's jealous of our mistress.

Madame PERNELLE
You hold your tongue, and think what you are saying.
He's not alone in censuring these visits;
The turmoil that attends your sort of people,
Their carriages forever at the door,
And all their noisy footmen, flocked together,
Annoy the neighbourhood, and raise a scandal.
I'd gladly think there's nothing really wrong;
But it makes talk; and that's not as it should be.

CLEANTE
Eh! madam, can you hope to keep folk's tongues
From wagging? It would be a grievous thing
If, for the fear of idle talk about us,
We had to sacrifice our friends. No, no;
Even if we could bring ourselves to do it,
Think you that everyone would then be silenced?
Against backbiting there is no defence
So let us try to live in innocence,
To silly tattle pay no heed at all,
And leave the gossips free to vent their gall.

DORINE
Our neighbour Daphne, and her little husband,
Must be the ones who slander us, I'm thinking.
Those whose own conduct's most ridiculous,

Are always quickest to speak ill of others;
They never fail to seize at once upon
The slightest hint of any love affair,
And spread the news of it with glee, and give it
The character they'd have the world believe in.
By others' actions, painted in their colours,
They hope to justify their own; they think,
In the false hope of some resemblance, either
To make their own intrigues seem innocent,
Or else to make their neighbours share the blame
Which they are loaded with by everybody.

Madame PERNELLE
These arguments are nothing to the purpose.
Orante, we all know, lives a perfect life;
Her thoughts are all of heaven; and I have heard
That she condemns the company you keep.

DORINE
O admirable pattern! Virtuous dame!
She lives the model of austerity;
But age has brought this piety upon her,
And she's a prude, now she can't help herself.
As long as she could capture men's attentions
She made the most of her advantages;
But, now she sees her beauty vanishing,
She wants to leave the world, that's leaving her,
And in the specious veil of haughty virtue
She'd hide the weakness of her worn-out charms.
That is the way with all your old coquettes;
They find it hard to see their lovers leave 'em;
And thus abandoned, their forlorn estate
Can find no occupation but a prude's.
These pious dames, in their austerity,
Must carp at everything, and pardon nothing.
They loudly blame their neighbours' way of living,
Not for religion's sake, but out of envy,
Because they can't endure to see another
Enjoy the pleasures age has weaned them from.

Madame PERNELLE [To **ELMIRE**]
There! That's the kind of rigmarole to please you,
Daughter-in-law. One never has a chance
To get a word in edgewise, at your house,
Because this lady holds the floor all day;
But none the less, I mean to have my say, too.
I tell you that my son did nothing wiser
In all his life, than take this godly man

Into his household; heaven sent him here,
In your great need, to make you all repent;
For your salvation, you must hearken to him;
He censures nothing but deserves his censure.
These visits, these assemblies, and these balls,
Are all inventions of the evil spirit.
You never hear a word of godliness
At them but idle cackle, nonsense, flimflam.
Our neighbour often comes in for a share,
The talk flies fast, and scandal fills the air;
It makes a sober person's head go round,
At these assemblies, just to hear the sound
Of so much gab, with not a word to say;
And as a learned man remarked one day
Most aptly, 'tis the Tower of Babylon,
Where all, beyond all limit, babble on.
And just to tell you how this point came in ...

[To **CLEANTE**]

So! Now the gentlemen must snicker, must he?
Go find fools like yourself to make you laugh
And don't ...

[To **ELMIRE**]

Daughter, good-bye; not one word more.
As for this house, I leave the half unsaid;
But I shan't soon set foot in it again,

[Cuffing **FLIPOTTE**.

Come, you! What makes you dream and stand agape,
Hussy! I'll warm your ears in proper shape!
March, trollop, march!

SCENE II

CLEANTE, DORINE.

CLEANTE

I won't escort her down,
For fear she might fall foul of me again;
The good old lady ...

DORINE

Bless us! What a pity
She shouldn't hear the way you speak of her!
She'd surely tell you you're too "good" by half,
And that she's not so "old" as all that, neither!

CLEANTE

How she got angry with us all for nothing!
And how she seems possessed with her Tartuffe!

DORINE

Her case is nothing, though, beside her son's!
To see him, you would say he's ten times worse!
His conduct in our late unpleasantness
Had won him much esteem, and proved his courage
In service of his king; but now he's like
A man besotted, since he's been so taken
With this Tartuffe. He calls him brother, loves him
A hundred times as much as mother, son,
Daughter, and wife. He tells him all his secrets
And lets him guide his acts, and rule his conscience.
He fondles and embraces him; a sweetheart
Could not, I think, be loved more tenderly;
At table he must have the seat of honour,
While with delight our master sees him eat
As much as six men could; we must give up
The choicest tidbits to him; if he belches,
('tis a servant speaking)
Master exclaims: "God bless you!" Oh, he dotes
Upon him! he's his universe, his hero;
He's lost in constant admiration, quotes him
On all occasions, takes his trifling acts
For wonders, and his words for oracles.
The fellow knows his dupe, and makes the most on't,
He fools him with a hundred masks of virtue,
Gets money from him all the time by canting,
And takes upon himself to carp at us.
Even his silly coxcomb of a lackey
Makes it his business to instruct us too;
He comes with rolling eyes to preach at us,
And throws away our ribbons, rouge, and patches.
The wretch, the other day, tore up a kerchief
That he had found, pressed in the Golden Legend,
Calling it a horrid crime for us to mingle
The devil's finery with holy things.

SCENE III

ELMIRE, MARIANE, DAMIS, CLEANTE, DORINE.

ELMIRE [to **CLEANTE**]

You're very lucky to have missed the speech
She gave us at the door. I see my husband
Is home again. He hasn't seen me yet,
So I'll go up and wait till he comes in.

CLEANTE
And I, to save time, will await him here;
I'll merely say good-morning, and be gone.

SCENE IV

CLEANTE, DAMIS, DORINE.

DAMIS
I wish you'd say a word to him about
My sister's marriage; I suspect Tartuffe
Opposes it, and puts my father up
To all these wretched shifts. You know, besides,
How nearly I'm concerned in it myself;
If love unites my sister and Valère,
I love his sister too; and if this marriage
Were to ...

DORINE
He's coming.

SCENE V

ORGON, CLEANTE, DORINE

ORGON
Ah! Good morning, brother.

CLEANTE
I was just going, but am glad to greet you.
Things are not far advanced yet, in the country?

ORGON
Dorine ...
[To **CLEANTE**]
Just wait a bit, please, brother-in-law.
Let me allay my first anxiety
By asking news about the family.
[To **DORINE**]

Has everything gone well these last two days?
What's happening? And how is everybody?

DORINE

Madam had fever, and a splitting headache
Day before yesterday, all day and evening.

ORGON

And how about Tartuffe?

DORINE

Tartuffe? He's well;
He's mighty well; stout, fat, fair, rosy-lipped.

ORGON

Poor man!

DORINE

At evening she had nausea
And couldn't touch a single thing for supper,
Her headache still was so severe.

ORGON

And how
About Tartuffe?

DORINE

He supped alone, before her,
And unctuously ate up two partridges,
As well as half a leg o' mutton, deviled.

ORGON

Poor man!

DORINE

All night she couldn't get a wink
Of sleep, the fever racked her so; and we
Had to sit up with her till daylight.

ORGON

How
About Tartuffe?

DORINE

Gently inclined to slumber,
He left the table, went into his room,
Got himself straight into a good warm bed,
And slept quite undisturbed until next morning.

ORGON
Poor man!

DORINE
At last she let us all persuade her,
And got up courage to be bled; and then
She was relieved at once.

ORGON
And how about
Tartuffe?

DORINE
He plucked up courage properly,
Bravely entrenched his soul against all evils,
And to replace the blood that she had lost,
He drank at breakfast four huge draughts of wine.

ORGON
Poor man!

DORINE
So now they both are doing well;
And I'll go straightway and inform my mistress
How pleased you are at her recovery.

SCENE VI

ORGON, CLEANTE.

CLEANTE
Brother, she ridicules you to your face;
And I, though I don't want to make you angry,
Must tell you candidly that she's quite right.
Was such infatuation ever heard of?
And can a man to-day have charms to make you
Forget all else, relieve his poverty,
Give him a home, and then ...?

ORGON
Stop there, good brother,
You do not know the man you're speaking of.

CLEANTE
Since you will have it so, I do not know him;

But after all, to tell what sort of man
He is ...

ORGON

Dear brother, you'd be charmed to know him;
Your raptures over him would have no end.
He is a man ... who ... ah! ... in fact ...a man
Whoever does his will, knows perfect peace,
And counts the whole world else, as so much dung.
His converse has transformed me quite; he weans
My heart from every friendship, teaches me
To have no love for anything on earth;
And I could see my brother, children, mother,
And wife, all die, and never care a snap.

CLEANTE

Your feelings are humane, I must say, brother!

ORGON

Ah! If you'd seen him, as I saw him first,
You would have loved him just as much as I.
He came to church each day, with contrite mien,
Kneeled, on both knees, right opposite my place,
And drew the eyes of all the congregation,
To watch the fervour of his prayers to heaven;
With deep-drawn sighs and great ejaculations,
He humbly kissed the earth at every moment;
And when I left the church, he ran before me
To give me holy water at the door.
I learned his poverty, and who he was,
By questioning his servant, who is like him,
And gave him gifts; but in his modesty
He always wanted to return a part.
"It is too much," he'd say, "too much by half;
I am not worthy of your pity." Then,
When I refused to take it back, he'd go,
Before my eyes, and give it to the poor.
At length heaven bade me take him to my home,
And since that day, all seems to prosper here.
He censures everything, and for my sake
He even takes great interest in my wife;
He lets me know who ogles her, and seems
Six times as jealous as I am myself.
You'd not believe how far his zeal can go:
He calls himself a sinner just for trifles;
The merest nothing is enough to shock him;
So much so, that the other day I heard him
Accuse himself for having, while at prayer,

In too much anger caught and killed a flea.

CLEANTE
Zounds, brother, you are mad, I think! Or else
You're making sport of me, with such a speech.
What are you driving at with all this nonsense ...?

ORGON
Brother, your language smacks of atheism;
And I suspect your soul's a little tainted
Therewith. I've preached to you a score of times
That you'll draw down some judgment on your head.

CLEANTE
That is the usual strain of all your kind;
They must have every one as blind as they.
They call you atheist if you have good eyes;
And if you don't adore their vain grimaces,
You've neither faith nor care for sacred things.
No, no; such talk can't frighten me; I know
What I am saying; heaven sees my heart.
We're not the dupes of all your canting mummers;
There are false heroes and false devotees;
And as true heroes never are the ones
Who make much noise about their deeds of honour,
Just so true devotees, whom we should follow,
Are not the ones who make so much vain show.
What! Will you find no difference between
Hypocrisy and genuine devoutness?
And will you treat them both alike, and pay
The self-same honour both to masks and faces
Set artifice beside sincerity,
Confuse the semblance with reality,
Esteem a phantom like a living person,
And counterfeit as good as honest coin?
Men, for the most part, are strange creatures, truly!
You never find them keep the golden mean;
The limits of good sense, too narrow for them,
Must always be passed by, in each direction;
They often spoil the noblest things, because
They go too far, and push them to extremes.
I merely say this by the way, good brother.

ORGON
You are the sole expounder of the doctrine;
Wisdom shall die with you, no doubt, good brother,
You are the only wise, the sole enlightened,
The oracle, the Cato, of our age.

All men, compared to you, are downright fools.

CLEANTE
I'm not the sole expounder of the doctrine,
And wisdom shall not die with me, good brother.
But this I know, though it be all my knowledge,
That there's a difference 'twixt false and true.
And as I find no kind of hero more
To be admired than men of true religion,
Nothing more noble or more beautiful
Than is the holy zeal of true devoutness;
Just so I think there's naught more odious
Than whited sepulchres of outward unction,
Those barefaced charlatans, those hireling zealots,
Whose sacrilegious, treacherous pretence
Deceives at will, and with impunity
Makes mockery of all that men hold sacred;
Men who, enslaved to selfish interests,
Make trade and merchandise of godliness,
And try to purchase influence and office
With false eye-rollings and affected raptures;
Those men, I say, who with uncommon zeal
Seek their own fortunes on the road to heaven;
Who, skilled in prayer, have always much to ask,
And live at court to preach retirement;
Who reconcile religion with their vices,
Are quick to anger, vengeful, faithless, tricky,
And, to destroy a man, will have the boldness
To call their private grudge the cause of heaven;
All the more dangerous, since in their anger
They use against us weapons men revere,
And since they make the world applaud their passion,
And seek to stab us with a sacred sword.
There are too many of this canting kind.
Still, the sincere are easy to distinguish;
And many splendid patterns may be found,
In our own time, before our very eyes
Look at Ariston, Periandre, Oronte,
Alcidamas, Clitandre, and Polydore;
No one denies their claim to true religion;
Yet they're no braggadocios of virtue,
They do not make insufferable display,
And their religion's human, tractable;
They are not always judging all our actions,
They'd think such judgment savoured of presumption;
And, leaving pride of words to other men,
'Tis by their deeds alone they censure ours.
Evil appearances find little credit

With them; they even incline to think the best
Of others. No caballers, no intriguers,
They mind the business of their own right living.
They don't attack a sinner tooth and nail,
For sin's the only object of their hatred;
Nor are they over-zealous to attempt
Far more in heaven's behalf than heaven would have 'em.
That is my kind of man, that is true living,
That is the pattern we should set ourselves.
Your fellow was not fashioned on this model;
You're quite sincere in boasting of his zeal;
But you're deceived, I think, by false pretences.

ORGON
My dear good brother-in-law, have you quite done?

CLEANTE
Yes.

ORGON
I'm your humble servant.

[Starts to go.

CLEANTE
Just a word.
We'll drop that other subject. But you know
Valère has had the promise of your daughter.

ORGON
Yes.

CLEANTE
You had named the happy day.

ORGON
'Tis true.

CLEANTE
Then why put off the celebration of it?

ORGON
I can't say.

CLEANTE
Can you have some other plan
In mind?

ORGON
Perhaps.

CLEANTE
You mean to break your word?

ORGON
I don't say that.

CLEANTE
I hope no obstacle
Can keep you from performing what you've promised.

ORGON
Well, that depends.

CLEANTE
Why must you beat about?
Valère has sent me here to settle matters.

ORGON
Heaven be praised!

CLEANTE
What answer shall I take him?

ORGON
Why, anything you please.

CLEANTE
But we must know
Your plans. What are they?

ORGON
I shall do the will
Of Heaven.

CLEANTE
Come, be serious. You've given
Your promise to Valère. Now will you keep it?

ORGON
Good-bye.

CLEANTE [alone]
His love, methinks, has much to fear;
I must go let him know what's happening here.

ACT II

SCENE I

ORGON, MARIANE.

ORGON
Now, Mariane.

MARIANE
Yes, father?

ORGON
Come; I'll tell you
A secret.

MARIANE
Yes ... What are you looking for?

ORGON [Looking into a small closet-room]
To see there's no one there to spy upon us;
That little closet's mighty fit to hide in.
There! We're all right now. Mariane, in you
I've always found a daughter dutiful
And gentle. So I've always love you dearly.

MARIANE
I'm grateful for your fatherly affection.

ORGON
Well spoken, daughter. Now, prove you deserve it
By doing as I wish in all respects.

MARIANE
To do so is the height of my ambition.

ORGON
Excellent well. What say you of Tartruffe?

MARIANE
Who? I?

ORGON
Yes, you. Look to it how you answer.

MARIANE

Why! I'll say of him anything you please.

SCENE II

ORGON, MARIANE, DORINE.

[Coming in quietly and standing behind **ORGON**, so that he does not see her.

ORGON
Well spoken. A good girl. Say then, my daughter,
That all his person shines with noble merit,
That he has won your heart, and you would like
To have him, by my choice, become your husband.
Eh?

MARIANE
Eh?

ORGON
What say you?

MARIANE
Please, what did you say?

ORGON
What?

MARIANE
Surely I mistook you, sir?

ORGON
How now?

MARIANE
Who is it, father, you would have me say
Has won my heart, and I would like to have
Become my husband, by your choice?

ORGON
Tartuffe.

MARIANE
But, father, I protest it isn't true!
Why should you make me tell this dreadful lie?

ORGON

Because I mean to have it be the truth.
Let this suffice for you: I've settled it.

MARIANE
What, father, you would ...?

ORGON
Yes, child, I'm resolved
To graft Tartuffe into my family.
So he must be your husband. That I've settled.
And since your duty...
[Seeing **DORINE**]
What are you doing there?
Your curiosity is keen, my girl,
To make you come eavesdropping on us so.

DORINE
Upon my word, I don't know how the rumour
Got started if 'twas guess-work or mere chance
But I had heard already of this match,
And treated it as utter stuff and nonsense.

ORGON
What! Is the thing incredible?

DORINE
So much so
I don't believe it even from yourself, sir.

ORGON
I know a way to make you credit it.

DORINE
No, no, you're telling us a fairly tale!

ORGON
I'm telling you just what will happen shortly.

DORINE
Stuff!

ORGON
Daughter, what I say is in good earnest.

DORINE
There, there, don't take your father seriously;
He's fooling.

ORGON
But I tell you ...

DORINE
No. No use.
They won't believe you.

ORGON
If I let my anger ...

DORINE
Well, then, we do believe you; and the worse
For you it is. What! Can a grown-up man
With that expanse of beard across his face
Be mad enough to want ...?

ORGON
You hark me:
You've taken on yourself here in this house
A sort of free familiarity
That I don't like, I tell you frankly, girl.

DORINE
There, there, let's not get angry, sir, I beg you.
But are you making game of everybody?
Your daughter's not cut out for bigot's meat;
And he has more important things to think of.
Besides, what can you gain by such a match?
How can a man of wealth, like you, go choose
A wretched vagabond for son-in-law?

ORGON
You hold your tongue. And know, the less he has,
The better cause have we to honour him.
His poverty is honest poverty;
It should exalt him more than worldly grandeur,
For he has let himself be robbed of all,
Through careless disregard of temporal things
And fixed attachment to the things eternal.
My help may set him on his feet again,
Win back his property a fair estate
He has at home, so I'm informed and prove him
For what he is, a true-born gentleman.

DORINE
Yes, so he says himself. Such vanity
But ill accords with pious living, sir.
The man who cares for holiness alone

Should not so loudly boast his name and birth;
The humble ways of genuine devoutness
Brook not so much display of earthly pride.
Why should he be so vain? ... But I offend you:
Let's leave his rank, then, take the man himself:
Can you without compunction give a man
Like him possession of a girl like her?
Think what a scandal's sure to come of it!
Virtue is at the mercy of the fates,
When a girl's married to a man she hates;
The best intent to live an honest woman
Depends upon the husband's being human,
And men whose brows are pointed at afar
May thank themselves their wives are what they are.
For to be true is more than woman can,
With husbands built upon a certain plan;
And he who weds his child against her will
Owes heaven account for it, if she do ill.
Think then what perils wait on your design.

ORGON [to **MARIANE**]
So! I must learn what's what from her, you see!

DORINE
You might do worse than follow my advice.

ORGON
Daughter, we can't waste time upon this nonsense;
I know what's good for you, and I'm your father.
True, I had promised you to young Valère;
But, first, they tell me he's inclined to gamble,
And then, I fear his faith is not quite sound.
I haven't noticed that he's regular
At church.

DORINE
You'd have him run there just when you do.
Like those who go on purpose to be seen?

ORGON
I don't ask your opinion on the matter.
In short, the other is in Heaven's best graces,
And that is riches quite beyond compare.
This match will bring you every joy you long for;
'Twill be all steeped in sweetness and delight.
You'll live together, in your faithful loves,
Like two sweet children, like two turtle-doves;
You'll never fail to quarrel, scold, or tease,

And you may do with him whate'er you please.

DORINE
With him? Do naught but give him horns, I'll warrant.

ORGON
Out on thee, wench!

DORINE
I tell you he's cut out for't;
However great your daughter's virtue, sir,
His destiny is sure to prove the stronger.

ORGON
Have done with interrupting. Hold your tongue.
Don't poke your nose in other people's business.

DORINE [She keeps interrupting him, just as he turns and starts to speak to his **DAUGHTER**]
If I make bold, sir, 'tis for your own good.

ORGON
You're too officious; pray you, hold your tongue.

DORINE
'Tis love of you ...

ORGON
I want none of your love.

DORINE
Then I will love you in your own despite.

ORGON
You will, eh?

DORINE
Yes, your honour's dear to me;
I can't endure to see you made the butt
Of all men's ridicule.

ORGON
Won't you be still?

DORINE
'Twould be a sin to let you make this match.

ORGON
Won't you be still, I say, you impudent viper!

DORINE

What! you are pious, and you lose your temper?

ORGON

I'm all wrought up, with your confounded nonsense;
Now, once for all, I tell you hold your tongue.

DORINE

Then mum's the word; I'll take it out in thinking.

ORGON

Think all you please; but not a syllable
To me about it, or ... you understand!
[Turning to his **DAUGHTER**]
As a wise father, I've considered all
With due deliberation.

DORINE

I'll go mad
If I can't speak.

[She stops the instant he turns his head.

ORGON

Though he's no lady's man,
TARTUFFE is well enough ...

DORINE

A pretty phiz!

ORGON

So that, although you may not care at all
For his best qualities ...

DORINE

A handsome dowry!

[**ORGON** turns and stands in front of her, with arms folded, eyeing her.
Were I in her place, any man should rue it
Who married me by force, that's mighty certain;
I'd let him know, and that within a week,
A woman's vengeance isn't far to seek.

ORGON [to **DORINE**]

So nothing that I say has any weight?

DORINE

Eh? What's wrong now? I didn't speak to you.

ORGON
What were you doing?

DORINE
Talking to myself.

ORGON
Oh! Very well. [Aside] Her monstrous impudence
Must be chastised with one good slap in the face.

[He stands ready to strike her, and, each time he speaks to his DAUGHTER, he glances toward her; but she stands still and says not a word.

ORGON
Daughter, you must approve of my design....
Think of this husband ... I have chosen for you...
[To **DORINE**]
Why don't you talk to yourself?

DORINE
Nothing to say.

ORGON
One little word more.

DORINE
Oh, no, thanks. Not now.

ORGON
Sure, I'd have caught you.

DORINE
Faith, I'm no such fool.

ORGON
So, daughter, now obedience is the word;
You must accept my choice with reverence.

DORINE [Running away]
You'd never catch me marrying such a creature.

ORGON [Swinging his hand at her and missing her]
Daughter, you've such a pestilent hussy there
I can't live with her longer, without sin.
I can't discuss things in the state I'm in.
My mind's so flustered by her insolent talk,

To calm myself, I must go take a walk.

SCENE III

MARIANE, DORINE.

DORINE
Say, have you lost the tongue from out your head?
And must I speak your rôle from A to Zed?
You let them broach a project that's absurd,
And don't oppose it with a single word!

MARIANE
What can I do? My father is the master.

DORINE
Do? Everything, to ward off such disaster.

MARIANE
But what?

DORINE
Tell him one doesn't love by proxy;
Tell him you'll marry for yourself, not him;
Since you're the one for whom the thing is done,
You are the one, not he, the man must please;
If his Tartuffe has charmed him so, why let him
Just marry him himself no one will hinder.

MARIANE
A father's rights are such, it seems to me,
That I could never dare to say a word.

DORINE
Came, talk it out. Valère has asked your hand:
Now do you love him, pray, or do you not?

MARIANE
DORINE! How can you wrong my love so much,
And ask me such a question? Have I not
A hundred times laid bare my heart to you?
Do you know how ardently I love him?

DORINE
How do I know if heart and words agree,
And if in honest truth you really love him?

MARIANE
Dorine, you wrong me greatly if you doubt it;
I've shown my inmost feelings, all too plainly.

DORINE
So then, you love him?

MARIANE
Yes, devotedly.

DORINE
And he returns your love, apparently?

MARIANE
I think so.

DORINE
And you both alike are eager
To be well married to each other?

MARIANE
Surely.

DORINE
Then what's your plan about this other match?

MARIANE
To kill myself, if it is forced upon me.

DORINE
Good! That's a remedy I hadn't thought of.
Just die, and everything will be all right.
This medicine is marvellous, indeed!
It drives me mad to hear folk talk such nonsense.

MARIANE
Oh dear, Dorine you get in such a temper!
You have no sympathy for people's troubles.

DORINE
I have no sympathy when folk talk nonsense,
And flatten out as you do, at a pinch.

MARIANE
But what can you expect? if one is timid?

DORINE

But what is love worth, if it has no courage?

MARIANE
Am I not constant in my love for him?
Is't not his place to win me from my father?

DORINE
But if your father is a crazy fool,
And quite bewitched with his Tartuffe? And breaks
His bounden word? Is that your lover's fault?

MARIANE
But shall I publicly refuse and scorn
This match, and make it plain that I'm in love?
Shall I cast off for him, whate'er he be,
Womanly modesty and filial duty?
You ask me to display my love in public ...?

DORINE
No, no, I ask you nothing. You shall be
Mister Tartuffe's; why, now I think of it,
I should be wrong to turn you from this marriage.
What cause can I have to oppose your wishes?
So fine a match! An excellent good match!
Mister Tartuffe! Oh ho! No mean proposal!
Mister Tartuffe, sure, take it all in all,
Is not a man to sneeze at oh, by no means!
'Tis no small luck to be his happy spouse.
The whole world joins to sing his praise already;
He's noble in his parish; handsome too;
Red ears and high complexion oh, my lud!
You'll be too happy, sure, with him for husband.

MARIANE
Oh dear! ...

DORINE
What joy and pride will fill your heart
To be the bride of such a handsome fellow!

MARIANE
Oh, stop, I beg you; try to find some way
To help break off the match. I quite give in,
I'm ready to do anything you say.

DORINE
No, no, a daughter must obey her father,
Though he should want to make her wed a monkey.

Besides, your fate is fine. What could be better!
You'll take the stage-coach to his little village,
And find it full of uncles and of cousins,
Whose conversation will delight you. Then
You'll be presented in their best society.
You'll even go to call, by way of welcome,
On Mrs. Bailiff, Mrs. Tax-Collector,
Who'll patronise you with a folding-stool.
There, once a year, at carnival, you'll have
Perhaps a ball; with orchestra two bag-pipes;
And sometimes a trained ape, and Punch and Judy;
Though if your husband ...

MARIANE
Oh, you'll kill me. Please
Contrive to help me out with your advice.

DORINE
I thank you kindly.

MARIANE
Oh! Dorine, I beg you ...

DORINE
To serve you right, this marriage must go through.

MARIANE
Dear girl!

DORINE
No.

MARIANE
If I say I love Valère ...

DORINE
No, no. Tartuffe's your man, and you shall taste him.

MARIANE
You know I've always trusted you; now help me ...

DORINE
No, you shall be, my faith! Tartuffified.

MARIANE
Well, then, since you've no pity for my fate
Let me take counsel only of despair;
It will advise and help and give me courage;

There's one sure cure, I know, for all my troubles.

[She starts to go.

DORINE
There, there! Come back. I can't be angry long.
I must take pity on you, after all.

MARIANE
Oh, don't you see, Dorine, if I must bear
This martyrdom, I certainly shall die.

DORINE
Now don't you fret. We'll surely find some way.
To hinder this ... But here's Valère, your lover.

SCENE IV

VALÈRE, MARIANE, DORINE.

VALÈRE
Madam, a piece of news quite new to me
Has just come out, and very fine it is.

MARIANE
What piece of news?

VALÈRE
Your marriage with Tartuffe.

MARIANE
'Tis true my father has this plan in mind.

VALÈRE
Your father, madam ...

MARIANE
Yes, he's changed his plans,
And did but now propose it to me.

VALÈRE
What!
Seriously?

MARIANE
Yes, he was serious,

And openly insisted on the match.

VALÈRE
And what's your resolution in the matter,
Madam?

MARIANE
I don't know.

VALÈRE
That's a pretty answer.
You don't know?

MARIANE
No.

VALÈRE
No?

MARIANE
What do you advise?

VALÈRE
I? My advice is, marry him, by all means.

MARIANE
That's your advice?

VALÈRE
Yes.

MARIANE
Do you mean it?

VALÈRE
Surely.
A splendid choice, and worthy of your acceptance.

MARIANE
Oh, very well, sir! I shall take your counsel.

VALÈRE
You'll find no trouble taking it, I warrant.

MARIANE
No more than you did giving it, be sure.

VALÈRE

I gave it, truly, to oblige you, madam.

MARIANE
And I shall take it to oblige you, sir.

DORINE [Withdrawing to the back of the stage]
Let's see what this affair will come to.

VALÈRE
So,
That is your love? And it was all deceit
When you ...

MARIANE
I beg you, say no more of that.
You told me, squarely, sir, I should accept
The husband that is offered me; and I
Will tell you squarely that I mean to do so,
Since you have given me this good advice.

VALÈRE
Don't shield yourself with talk of my advice.
You had your mind made up, that's evident;
And now you're snatching at a trifling pretext
To justify the breaking of your word.

MARIANE
Exactly so.

VALÈRE
Of course it is; your heart
Has never known true love for me.

MARIANE
Alas!
You're free to think so, if you please.

VALÈRE
Yes, yes,
I'm free to think so; and my outraged love
May yet forestall you in your perfidy,
And offer elsewhere both my heart and hand.

MARIANE
No doubt of it; the love your high deserts
May win ...

VALÈRE

Good Lord, have done with my deserts!
I know I have but few, and you have proved it.
But I may find more kindness in another;
I know of someone, who'll not be ashamed
To take your leavings, and make up my loss.

MARIANE

The loss is not so great; you'll easily
Console yourself completely for this change.

VALÈRE

I'll try my best, that you may well believe.
When we're forgotten by a woman's heart,
Our pride is challenged; we, too, must forget;
Or if we cannot, must at least pretend to.
No other way can man such baseness prove,
As be a lover scorned, and still in love.

MARIANE

In faith, a high and noble sentiment.

VALÈRE

Yes; and it's one that all men must approve.
What! Would you have me keep my love alive,
And see you fly into another's arms
Before my very eyes; and never offer
To someone else the heart that you had scorned?

MARIANE

Oh, no, indeed! For my part, I could wish
That it were done already.

VALÈRE

What! You wish it?

MARIANE

Yes.

VALÈRE

This is insult heaped on injury;
I'll go at once and do as you desire.

[He takes a step or two as if to go away.

MARIANE

Oh, very well then.

VALÈRE [Turning back]

But remember this.
'Twas you that drove me to this desperate pass.

MARIANE
Of course.

VALÈRE [Turning back again]
And in the plan that I have formed
I only follow your example.

MARIANE
Yes.

VALÈRE [At the door]
Enough; you shall be punctually obeyed.

MARIANE
So much the better.

VALÈRE [Coming back again]
This is once for all.

MARIANE
So be it, then.

VALÈRE [He goes toward the door, but just as he reaches it, turns around]
Eh?

MARIANE
What?

VALÈRE
You didn't call me?

MARIANE
I? You are dreaming.

VALÈRE
Very well, I'm gone. Madam, farewell.

[He walks slowly away.

MARIANE
Farewell, sir.

DORINE
I must say
You've lost your senses and both gone clean daft!

I've let you fight it out to the end o' the chapter
To see how far the thing could go. Oho, there,
Mister Valère!

[She goes and seizes him by the arm, to stop him. He makes a great show of resistance.

VALÈRE
What do you want, Dorine?

DORINE
Come here.

VALÈRE
No, no, I'm quite beside myself.
Don't hinder me from doing as she wishes.

DORINE
Stop!

VALÈRE
No. You see, I'm fixed, resolved, determined.

DORINE
So!

MARIANE [Aside]
Since my presence pains him, makes him go,
I'd better go myself, and leave him free.

DORINE [Leaving **VALÈRE**, and running after **MARIANE**]
Now t'other! Where are you going?

MARIANE
Let me be.

DORINE.
Come back.

MARIANE
No, no, it isn't any use.

VALÈRE [aside]
'Tis clear the sight of me is torture to her;
No doubt, t'were better I should free her from it.

DORINE [Leaving **MARIANE** and running after **VALÈRE**]
Same thing again! Deuce take you both, I say.
Now stop your fooling; come here, you; and you.

[She pulls first one, then the other, toward the middle of the stage.

VALÈRE [To **DORINE**]
What's your idea?

MARIANE [To **DORINE**]
What can you mean to do?

DORINE
Set you to rights, and pull you out o' the scrape.
[To **VALÈRE**]
Are you quite mad, to quarrel with her now?

VALÈRE
Didn't you hear the things she said to me?

DORINE [to **MARIANE**]
Are you quite mad, to get in such a passion?

MARIANE
Didn't you see the way he treated me?

DORINE
Fools, both of you.
[To **VALÈRE**]
She thinks of nothing else
But to keep faith with you, I vouch for it.
[To **MARIANE**]
And he loves none but you, and longs for nothing
But just to marry you, I stake my life on't.

MARIANE [To **VALÈRE**]
Why did you give me such advice then, pray?

VALÈRE [To **MARIANE**]
Why ask for my advice on such a matter?

DORINE
You both are daft, I tell you. Here, your hands.
[To **VALÈRE**]
Come, yours.

VALÈRE [Giving **DORINE** his hand]
What for?

DORINE [To **MARIANE**]
Now, yours.

MARIANE [Giving **DORINE** her hand]
But what's the use?

DORINE
Oh, quick now, come along. There, both of you
You love each other better than you think.

[**VALÈRE** and **MARIANE** hold each other's hands some time without looking at each other.

VALÈRE [At last turning toward **MARIANE**]
Come, don't be so ungracious now about it;
Look at a man as if you didn't hate him.

[**MARIANE** looks sideways toward **VALÈRE**, with just a bit of a smile.

DORINE
My faith and troth, what fools these lovers be!

VALÈRE [To **MARIANE**]
But come now, have I not a just complaint?
And truly, are you not a wicked creature
To take delight in saying what would pain me?

MARIANE
And are you not yourself the most ungrateful ...?

DORINE
Leave this discussion till another time;
Now, think how you'll stave off this plaguy marriage.

MARIANE
Then tell us how to go about it.

DORINE
Well,
We'll try all sorts of ways.
[To **MARIANE**]
Your father's daft;
[To **VALÈRE**]
This plan is nonsense.
[To **MARIANE**]
You had better humour
His notions by a semblance of consent,
So that in case of danger, you can still
Find means to block the marriage by delay.
If you gain time, the rest is easy, trust me.
One day you'll fool them with a sudden illness,

Causing delay; another day, ill omens:
You've met a funeral, or broke a mirror,
Or dreamed of muddy water. Best of all,
They cannot marry you to anyone
Without your saying yes. But now, methinks,
They mustn't find you chattering together.
[To **VALÈRE**]
You, go at once and set your friends at work
To make him keep his word to you; while we
Will bring the brother's influence to bear,
And get the step-mother on our side, too.
Good-bye.

VALÈRE [To **MARIANE**]
Whatever efforts we may make,
My greatest hope, be sure, must rest on you.

MARIANE [To **VALÈRE**]
I cannot answer for my father's whims;
But no one save Valère shall ever have me.

VALÈRE
You thrill me through with joy! Whatever comes ...

DORINE
Oho! These lovers! Never done with prattling!
Now go.

VALÈRE [Starting to go, and coming back again]
One last word ...

DORINE
What a gabble and pother!
Be off! By this door, you. And you, by t'other.

[She pushes them off, by the shoulders, in opposite directions.

ACT III

SCENE I

DAMIS, DORINE.

DAMIS
May lightning strike me dead this very instant,
May I be everywhere proclaimed a scoundrel,

If any reverence or power shall stop me,
And if I don't do straightway something desperate!

DORINE

I beg you, moderate this towering passion;
Your father did but merely mention it.
Not all things that are talked of turn to facts;
The road is long, sometimes, from plans to acts.

DAMIS

No, I must end this paltry fellow's plots,
And he shall hear from me a truth or two.

DORINE

So ho! Go slow now. Just you leave the fellow
Your father too in your step-mother's hands.
She has some influence with this Tartuffe,
He makes a point of heeding all she says,
And I suspect that he is fond of her.
Would God 'twere true! 'Twould be the height of humour
Now, she has sent for him, in your behalf,
To sound him on this marriage, to find out
What his ideas are, and to show him plainly
What troubles he may cause, if he persists
In giving countenance to this design.
His man says, he's at prayers, I mustn't see him,
But likewise says, he'll presently be down.
So off with you, and let me wait for him.

DAMIS

I may be present at this interview.

DORINE

No, no! They must be left alone.

DAMIS

I won't
So much as speak to him.

DORINE

Go on! We know you
And your high tantrums. Just the way to spoil things!
Be off.

DAMIS

No, I must see I'll keep my temper.

DORINE
Out on you, what a plague! He's coming. Hide!

[**DAMIS** goes and hides in the closet at the back of the stage.

SCENE II

TARTUFFE, DORINE

TARTUFFE [Speaking to his **VALET**, off the stage, as soon as he sees **DORINE** is there]
Lawrence, put up my hair-cloth shirt and scourge,
And pray that Heaven may shed its light upon you.
If any come to see me, say I'm gone
To share my alms among the prisoners.

DORINE [aside]
What affectation and what showing off!

TARTUFFE What do you want with me?

DORINE
To tell you ...

TARTUFFE [taking a handkerchief from his pocket]
Ah!
Before you speak, pray take this handkerchief.

DORINE
What?

TARTUFFE
Cover up that bosom, which I can't
Endure to look on. Things like that offend
Our souls, and fill our minds with sinful thoughts.

DORINE
Are you so tender to temptation, then,
And has the flesh such power upon your senses?
I don't know how you get in such a heat;
For my part, I am not so prone to lust,
And I could see you stripped from head to foot,
And all your hide not tempt me in the least.

TARTUFFE
Show in your speech some little modesty,
Or I must instantly take leave of you.

DORINE
No, no, I'll leave you to yourself; I've only
One thing to say: Madam will soon be down,
And begs the favour of a word with you.

TARTUFFE
Ah! Willingly.

DORINE [Aside]
How gentle all at once!
My faith, I still believe I've hit upon it.

TARTUFFE
Will she come soon?

DORINE
I think I hear her now.
Yes, here she is herself; I'll leave you with her.

SCENE III

ELMIRE, TARTUFFE.

TARTUFFE
May Heaven's overflowing kindness ever
Give you good health of body and of soul,
And bless your days according to the wishes
And prayers of its most humble votary!

ELMIRE
I'm very grateful for your pious wishes.
But let's sit down, so we may talk at ease.

TARTUFFE [After sitting down]
And how are you recovered from your illness?

ELMIRE [sitting down also]
Quite well; the fever soon let go its hold.

TARTUFFE
My prayers, I fear, have not sufficient merit
To have drawn down this favour from on high;
But each entreaty that I made to Heaven
Had for its object your recovery.

ELMIRE
You're too solicitous on my behalf.

TARTUFFE
We could not cherish your dear health too much;
I would have given mine, to help restore it.

ELMIRE
That's pushing Christian charity too far;
I owe you many thanks for so much kindness.

TARTUFFE
I do far less for you than you deserve.

ELMIRE
There is a matter that I wished to speak of
In private; I am glad there's no one here
To listen.

TARTUFFE
Madam, I am overjoyed.
'Tis sweet to find myself alone with you.
This is an opportunity I've asked
Of Heaven, many a time; till now, in vain.

ELMIRE
All that I wish, is just a word from you,
Quite frank and open, hiding nothing from me.

[**DAMIS**, without their seeing him, opens the closet door halfway.

TARTUFFE
I too could wish, as Heaven's especial favour,
To lay my soul quite open to your eyes,
And swear to you, the trouble that I made
About those visits which your charms attract,
Does not result from any hatred toward you,
But rather from a passionate devotion,
And purest motives ...

ELMIRE
That is how I take it,
I think 'tis my salvation that concerns you.

TARTUFFE [pressing her finger tips]
Madam, 'tis so; and such is my devotion ...

ELMIRE

Ouch! but you squeeze too hard.

TARTUFFE
Excess of zeal.
In no way could I ever mean to hurt you,
And I'd as soon ...

[He puts his hand on her knee.

ELMIRE
What's your hand doing there?

TARTUFFE
Feeling your gown; the stuff is very soft.

ELMIRE
Let be, I beg you; I am very ticklish.

[She moves her chair away, and **TARTUFFE** brings his nearer.

TARTUFFE [handling the lace yoke of **ELMIRE**'s dress]
Dear me how wonderful in workmanship
This lace is! They do marvels, nowadays;
Things of all kinds were never better made.

ELMIRE
Yes, very true. But let us come to business.
They say my husband means to break his word.
And marry Mariane to you. Is't so?

TARTUFFE
He did hint some such thing; but truly, madam,
That's not the happiness I'm yearning after;
I see elsewhere the sweet compelling charms
Of such a joy as fills my every wish.

ELMIRE
You mean you cannot love terrestrial things.

TARTUFFE
The heart within my bosom is not stone.

ELMIRE
I well believe your sighs all tend to Heaven,
And nothing here below can stay your thoughts.

TARTUFFE
Love for the beauty of eternal things

Cannot destroy our love for earthly beauty;
Our mortal senses well may be entranced
By perfect works that Heaven has fashioned here.
Its charms reflected shine in such as you,
And in yourself, its rarest miracles;
It has displayed such marvels in your face,
That eyes are dazed, and hearts are rapt away;
I could not look on you, the perfect creature,
Without admiring Nature's great Creator,
And feeling all my heart inflamed with love
For you, His fairest image of Himself.
At first I trembled lest this secret love
Might be the Evil Spirit's artful snare;
I even schooled my heart to flee your beauty,
Thinking it was a bar to my salvation.
But soon, enlightened, O all lovely one,
I saw how this my passion may be blameless,
How I may make it fit with modesty,
And thus completely yield my heart to it.
'Tis I must own, a great presumption in me
To dare make you the offer of my heart;
My love hopes all things from your perfect goodness,
And nothing from my own poor weak endeavour.
You are my hope, my stay, my peace of heart;
On you depends my torment or my bliss;
And by your doom of judgment, I shall be
Blest, if you will; or damned, by your decree.

ELMIRE

Your declaration's turned most gallantly;
But truly, it is just a bit surprising.
You should have better armed your heart, methinks,
And taken thought somewhat on such a matter.
A pious man like you, known everywhere ...

TARTUFFE

Though pious, I am none the less a man;
And when a man beholds your heavenly charms,
The heart surrenders, and can think no more.
I know such words seem strange, coming from me;
But, madam, I'm no angel, after all;
If you condemn my frankly made avowal
You only have your charming self to blame.
Soon as I saw your more than human beauty,
You were thenceforth the sovereign of my soul;
Sweetness ineffable was in your eyes,
That took by storm my still resisting heart,
And conquered everything, fasts, prayers, and tears,

And turned my worship wholly to yourself.
My looks, my sighs, have spoke a thousand times;
Now, to express it all, my voice must speak.
If but you will look down with gracious favour
Upon the sorrows of your worthless slave,
If in your goodness you will give me comfort
And condescend unto my nothingness,
I'll ever pay you, O sweet miracle,
An unexampled worship and devotion.
Then too, with me your honour runs no risk;
With me you need not fear a public scandal.
These court gallants, that women are so fond of,
Are boastful of their acts, and vain in speech;
They always brag in public of their progress;
Soon as a favour's granted, they'll divulge it;
Their tattling tongues, if you but trust to them,
Will foul the altar where their hearts have worshipped.
But men like me are so discreet in love,
That you may trust their lasting secrecy.
The care we take to guard our own good name
May fully guarantee the one we love;
So you may find, with hearts like ours sincere,
Love without scandal, pleasure without fear.

ELMIRE
I've heard you through your speech is clear, at least.
But don't you fear that I may take a fancy
To tell my husband of your gallant passion,
And that a prompt report of this affair
May somewhat change the friendship which he bears you?

TARTUFFE
I know that you're too good and generous,
That you will pardon my temerity,
Excuse, upon the score of human frailty,
The violence of passion that offends you,
And not forget, when you consult your mirror,
That I'm not blind, and man is made of flesh.

ELMIRE
Some women might do otherwise, perhaps,
But I am willing to employ discretion,
And not repeat the matter to my husband;
But in return, I'll ask one thing of you:
That you urge forward, frankly and sincerely,
The marriage of Valère to Mariane;
That you give up the unjust influence
By which you hope to win another's rights;

And ...

ELMIRE, DAMIS, TARTUFFE.

DAMIS [Coming out of the closet-room where he had been hiding]
No, I say! This thing must be made public.
I was just there, and overheard it all;
And Heaven's goodness must have brought me there
On purpose to confound this scoundrel's pride
And grant me means to take a signal vengeance
On his hypocrisy and arrogance,
And undeceive my father, showing up
The rascal caught at making love to you.

ELMIRE
No, no; it is enough if he reforms,
Endeavouring to deserve the favour shown him.
And since I've promised, do not you belie me.
'Tis not my way to make a public scandal;
An honest wife will scorn to heed such follies,
And never fret her husband's ears with them.

DAMIS
You've reasons of your own for acting thus;
And I have mine for doing otherwise.
To spare him now would be a mockery;
His bigot's pride has triumphed all too long
Over my righteous anger, and has caused
Far too much trouble in our family.
The rascal all too long has ruled my father,
And crossed my sister's love, and mine as well.
The traitor now must be unmasked before him:
And Providence has given me means to do it.
To Heaven I owe the opportunity,
And if I did not use it now I have it,
I should deserve to lose it once for all.

ELMIRE
Damis ...

DAMIS
No, by your leave; I'll not be counselled.
I'm overjoyed. You needn't try to tell me
I must give up the pleasure of revenge.

I'll make an end of this affair at once;
And, to content me, here's my father now.

SCENE V

ORGON, ELMIRE, DAMIS, TARTUFFE.

DAMIS
Father, we've news to welcome your arrival,
That's altogether novel, and surprising.
You are well paid for your caressing care,
And this fine gentleman rewards your love
Most handsomely, with zeal that seeks no less
Than your dishonour, as has now been proven.
I've just surprised him making to your wife
The shameful offer of a guilty love.
She, somewhat over gentle and discreet,
Insisted that the thing should be concealed;
But I will not condone such shamelessness,
Nor so far wrong you as to keep it secret.

ELMIRE
Yes, I believe a wife should never trouble
Her husband's peace of mind with such vain gossip;
A woman's honour does not hang on telling;
It is enough if she defend herself;
Or so I think; Damis, you'd not have spoken,
If you would but have heeded my advice.

SCENE VI

ORGON, DAMIS, TARTUFFE.

ORGON
Just Heaven! Can what I hear be credited?

TARTUFFE
Yes, brother, I am wicked, I am guilty,
A miserable sinner, steeped in evil,
The greatest criminal that ever lived.
Each moment of my life is stained with soilures;
And all is but a mass of crime and filth;
Heaven, for my punishment, I see it plainly,
Would mortify me now. Whatever wrong

They find to charge me with, I'll not deny it
But guard against the pride of self-defence.
Believe their stories, arm your wrath against me,
And drive me like a villain from your house;
I cannot have so great a share of shame
But what I have deserved a greater still.

ORGON [To his **SON**]
You miscreant, can you dare, with such a falsehood,
To try to stain the whiteness of his virtue?

DAMIS
What! The feigned meekness of this hypocrite
Makes you discredit ...

ORGON
Silence, cursed plague!

TARTUFFE
Ah! Let him speak; you chide him wrongfully;
You'd do far better to believe his tales.
Why favour me so much in such a matter?
How can you know of what I'm capable?
And should you trust my outward semblance, brother,
Or judge therefrom that I'm the better man?
No, no; you let appearances deceive you;
I'm anything but what I'm thought to be,
Alas! and though all men believe me godly,
The simple truth is, I'm a worthless creature.
[To **DAMIS**]
Yes, my dear son, say on, and call me traitor,
Abandoned scoundrel, thief, and murderer;
Heap on me names yet more detestable,
And I shall not gainsay you; I've deserved them;
I'll bear this ignominy on my knees,
To expiate in shame the crimes I've done.

ORGON [To **TARTUFFE**]
Ah, brother, 'tis too much!
[To his **SON**]
You'll not relent,
You blackguard?

DAMIS
What! His talk can so deceive you ...

ORGON
Silence, you scoundrel!

[To **TARTUFFE**]
Brother, rise, I beg you.
[To his **SON**]
Infamous villain!

DAMIS
Can he ...

ORGON
Silence!

DAMIS
What ...

ORGON
Another word, I'll break your every bone.

TARTUFFE
Brother, in God's name, don't be angry with him!
I'd rather bear myself the bitterest torture
Than have him get a scratch on my account.

ORGON [To his **SON**]
Ungrateful monster!

TARTUFFE
Stop. Upon my knees
I beg you pardon him ...

ORGON [Throwing himself on his knees too, and embracing **TARTUFFE**]
Alas! How can you?
[To his **SON**]
Villain! Behold his goodness!

DAMIS
So ...

ORGON
Be still.

DAMIS
What! I ...

ORGON
Be still, I say. I know your motives
For this attack. You hate him, all of you;
Wife, children, servants, all let loose upon him,
You have recourse to every shameful trick

To drive this godly man out of my house;
The more you strive to rid yourselves of him,
The more I'll strive to make him stay with me;
I'll have him straightway married to my daughter,
Just to confound the pride of all of you.

DAMIS
What! Will you force her to accept his hand?

ORGON
Yes, and this very evening, to enrage you,
Young rascal! Ah! I'll brave you all, and show you
That I'm the master, and must be obeyed.
Now, down upon your knees this instant, rogue,
And take back what you said, and ask his pardon.

DAMIS
Who? I? Ask pardon of that cheating scoundrel ...?

ORGON
Do you resist, you beggar, and insult him?
A cudgel, here! a cudgel!
[To **TARTUFFE**]
Don't restrain me.
[To his **SON**]
Off with you! Leave my house this instant, sirrah,
And never dare set foot in it again.

DAMIS
Yes, I will leave your house, but ...

ORGON
Leave it quickly.
You reprobate, I disinherit you,
And give you, too, my curse into the bargain.

SCENE VII

ORGON, TARTUFFE.

ORGON
What! So insult a saintly man of God!

TARTUFFE
Heaven, forgive him all the pain he gives me!
[To **ORGON**]

Could you but know with what distress I see
Them try to vilify me to my brother!

ORGON
Ah!

TARTUFFE
The mere thought of such ingratitude
Makes my soul suffer torture, bitterly ...
My horror at it ... Ah! my heart's so full
I cannot speak ... I think I'll die of it.

ORGON [In tears, running to the door through which he drove away his **SON**]
Scoundrel! I wish I'd never let you go,
But slain you on the spot with my own hand.
[To **TARTUFFE**]
Brother, compose yourself, and don't be angry.

TARTUFFE
Nay, brother, let us end these painful quarrels.
I see what troublous times I bring upon you,
And think 'tis needful that I leave this house.

ORGON
What! You can't mean it?

TARTUFFE
Yes, they hate me here,
And try, I find, to make you doubt my faith.

ORGON
What of it? Do you find I listen to them?

TARTUFFE
No doubt they won't stop there. These same reports
You now reject, may some day win a hearing.

ORGON
No, brother, never.

TARTUFFE
Ah! my friend, a woman
May easily mislead her husband's mind.

ORGON
No, no.

TARTUFFE

So let me quickly go away
And thus remove all cause for such attacks.

ORGON
No, you shall stay; my life depends upon it.

TARTUFFE
Then I must mortify myself. And yet,
If you should wish ...

ORGON
No, never!

TARTUFFE
Very well, then;
No more of that. But I shall rule my conduct
To fit the case. Honour is delicate,
And friendship binds me to forestall suspicion,
Prevent all scandal, and avoid your wife.

ORGON
No, you shall haunt her, just to spite them all.
'Tis my delight to set them in a rage;
You shall be seen together at all hours
And what is more, the better to defy them,
I'll have no other heir but you; and straightway
I'll go and make a deed of gift to you,
Drawn in due form, of all my property.
A good true friend, my son-in-law to be,
Is more to me than son, and wife, and kindred.
You will accept my offer, will you not?

TARTUFFE
Heaven's will be done in everything!

ORGON
Poor man!
We'll go make haste to draw the deed aright,
And then let envy burst itself with spite!

ACT IV

SCENE I

CLEANTE, TARTUFFE.

CLEANTE

Yes, it's become the talk of all the town,
And make a stir that's scarcely to your credit;
And I have met you, sir, most opportunely,
To tell you in a word my frank opinion.
Not to sift out this scandal to the bottom,
Suppose the worst for us suppose Damis
Acted the traitor, and accused you falsely;
Should not a Christian pardon this offence,
And stifle in his heart all wish for vengeance?
Should you permit that, for your petty quarrel,
A son be driven from his father's house?
I tell you yet again, and tell you frankly,
Everyone, high or low, is scandalised;
If you'll take my advice, you'll make it up,
And not push matters to extremities.
Make sacrifice to God of your resentment;
Restore the son to favour with his father.

TARTUFFE

Alas! So far as I'm concerned, how gladly
Would I do so! I bear him no ill will;
I pardon all, lay nothing to his charge,
And wish with all my heart that I might serve him;
But Heaven's interests cannot allow it;
If he returns, then I must leave the house.
After his conduct, quite unparalleled,
All intercourse between us would bring scandal;
God knows what everyone's first thought would be!
They would attribute it to merest scheming
On my part say that conscious of my guilt
I feigned a Christian love for my accuser,
But feared him in my heart, and hoped to win him
And underhandedly secure his silence.

CLEANTE

You try to put us off with specious phrases;
But all your arguments are too far-fetched.
Why take upon yourself the cause of Heaven?
Does Heaven need our help to punish sinners?
Leave to itself the care of its own vengeance,
And keep in mind the pardon it commands us;
Besides, think somewhat less of men's opinions,
When you are following the will of Heaven.
Shall petty fear of what the world may think
Prevent the doing of a noble deed?
No! let us always do as Heaven commands,
And not perplex our brains with further questions.

TARTUFFE

Already I have told you I forgive him;
And that is doing, sir, as Heaven commands.
But after this day's scandal and affront
Heaven does not order me to live with him.

CLEANTE

And does it order you to lend your ear
To what mere whim suggested to his father,
And to accept gift of his estates,
On which, in justice, you can make no claim?

TARTUFFE

No one who knows me, sir, can have the thought
That I am acting from a selfish motive.
The goods of this world have no charms for me;
I am not dazzled by their treacherous glamour;
And if I bring myself to take the gift
Which he insists on giving me, I do so,
To tell the truth, only because I fear
This whole estate may fall into bad hands,
And those to whom it comes may use it ill
And not employ it, as is my design,
For Heaven's glory and my neighbours' good.

CLEANTE

Eh, sir, give up these conscientious scruples
That well may cause a rightful heir's complaints.
Don't take so much upon yourself, but let him
Possess what's his, at his own risk and peril;
Consider, it were better he misused it,
Than you should be accused of robbing him.
I am astounded that unblushingly
You could allow such offers to be made!
Tell me has true religion any maxim
That teaches us to rob the lawful heir?
If Heaven has made it quite impossible
Damis and you should live together here,
Were it not better you should quietly
And honourably withdraw, than let the son
Be driven out for your sake, dead against
All reason? 'Twould be giving, sir, believe me,
Such an example of your probity ...

TARTUFFE

Sir, it is half-past three; certain devotions
Recall me to my closet; you'll forgive me

For leaving you so soon.

CLEANTE [Alone]
Ah!

SCENE II

ELMIRE, MARIANE, CLEANTE, DORINE.

DORINE [To **CLEANTE**]
Sir, we beg you
To help us all you can in her behalf;
She's suffering almost more than heart can bear;
This match her father means to make to-night
Drives her each moment to despair. He's coming.
Let us unite our efforts now, we beg you,
And try by strength or skill to change his purpose.

SCENE III

ORGON, ELMIRE, MARIANE, CLEANTE, DORINE.

ORGON
So ho! I'm glad to find you all together.
[To **MARIANE**]
Here is the contract that shall make you happy,
My dear. You know already what it means.

MARIANE [On her knees before **ORGON**]
Father, I beg you, in the name of Heaven
That knows my grief, and by whate'er can move you,
Relax a little your paternal rights,
And free my love from this obedience!
Oh, do not make me, by your harsh command,
Complain to Heaven you ever were my father;
Do not make wretched this poor life you gave me.
If, crossing that fond hope which I had formed,
You'll not permit me to belong to one
Whom I have dared to love, at least, I beg you
Upon my knees, oh, save me from the torment
Of being possessed by one whom I abhor!
And do not drive me to some desperate act
By exercising all your rights upon me.

ORGON [A little touched]
Come, come, my heart, be firm! no human weakness!

MARIANE
I am not jealous of your love for him;
Display it freely; give him your estate,
And if that's not enough, add all of mine;
I willingly agree, and give it up,
If only you'll not give him me, your daughter;
Oh, rather let a convent's rigid rule
Wear out the wretched days that Heaven allots me.

ORGON
These girls are ninnies! always turning nuns
When fathers thwart their silly love-affairs.
Get on your feet! The more you hate to have him,
The more 'twill help you earn your soul's salvation.
So, mortify your senses by this marriage,
And don't vex me about it any more.

DORINE
But what ...?

ORGON
You hold your tongue, before your betters.
Don't dare to say a single word, I tell you.

CLEANTE
If you will let me answer, and advise ...

ORGON
Brother, I value your advice most highly;
'Tis well thought out; no better can be had;
But you'll allow me not to follow it.

ELMIRE [To her **HUSBAND**]
I can't find words to cope with such a case;
Your blindness makes me quite astounded at you.
You are bewitched with him, to disbelieve
The things we tell you happened here to-day.

ORGON
I am your humble servant, and can see
Things, when they're plain as noses on folks' faces,
I know you're partial to my rascal son,
And didn't dare to disavow the trick
He tried to play on this poor man; besides,
You were too calm, to be believed; if that

Had happened, you'd have been far more disturbed.

ELMIRE
And must our honour always rush to arms
At the mere mention of illicit love?
Or can we answer no attack upon it
Except with blazing eyes and lips of scorn?
For my part, I just laugh away such nonsense;
I've no desire to make a loud to-do.
Our virtue should, I think, be gentle-natured;
Nor can I quite approve those savage prudes
Whose honour arms itself with teeth and claws
To tear men's eyes out at the slightest word.
Heaven preserve me from that kind of honour!
I like my virtue not to be a vixen,
And I believe a quiet cold rebuff
No less effective to repulse a lover.

ORGON
I know ... and you can't throw me off the scent.

ELMIRE
Once more, I am astounded at your weakness;
I wonder what your unbelief would answer,
If I should let you see we've told the truth?

ORGON
See it?

ELMIRE
Yes.

ORGON
Nonsense.

ELMIRE
Come! If I should find
A way to make you see it clear as day?

ORGON
All rubbish.

ELMIRE
What a man! But answer me.
I'm not proposing now that you believe us;
But let's suppose that here, from proper hiding,
You should be made to see and hear all plainly;
What would you say then, to your man of virtue?

ORGON

Why, then, I'd say ... say nothing. It can't be.

ELMIRE

Your error has endured too long already,
And quite too long you've branded me a liar.
I must at once, for my own satisfaction,
Make you a witness of the things we've told you.

ORGON

Amen! I take you at your word. We'll see
What tricks you have, and how you'll keep your promise.

ELMIRE [To **DORINE**]

Send him to me.

DORINE [To **ELMIRE**]

The man's a crafty codger,
Perhaps you'll find it difficult to catch him.

ELMIRE [To **DORINE**]

Oh no! A lover's never hard to cheat,
And self-conceit leads straight to self-deceit.
Bid him come down to me.
[To **CLEANTE** and **MARIANE**]
And you, withdraw.

SCENE IV

ELMIRE, ORGON.

ELMIRE

Bring up this table, and get under it.

ORGON

What?

ELMIRE

One essential is to hide you well.

ORGON

Why under there?

ELMIRE

Oh, dear! Do as I say;

I know what I'm about, as you shall see.
Get under, now, I tell you; and once there
Be careful no one either sees or hears you.

ORGON
I'm going a long way to humour you,
I must say; but I'll see you through your scheme.

ELMIRE
And then you'll have, I think, no more to say.
[To her **HUSBAND**, who is now under the table]
But mind, I'm going to meddle with strange matters;
Prepare yourself to be in no wise shocked.
Whatever I may say must pass, because
'Tis only to convince you, as I promised.
By wheedling speeches, since I'm forced to do it,
I'll make this hypocrite put off his mask,
Flatter the longings of his shameless passion,
And give free play to all his impudence.
But, since 'tis for your sake, to prove to you
His guilt, that I shall feign to share his love,
I can leave off as soon as you're convinced,
And things shall go no farther than you choose.
So, when you think they've gone quite far enough,
It is for you to stop his mad pursuit,
To spare your wife, and not expose me farther
Than you shall need, yourself, to undeceive you.
It is your own affair, and you must end it
When ... Here he comes. Keep still, don't show yourself.

SCENE V

TARTUFFE, ELMIRE, ORGON, under the table,

TARTUFFE
They told me that you wished to see me here.

ELMIRE
Yes. I have secrets for your ear alone.
But shut the door first, and look everywhere
For fear of spies.

[**TARTUFFE** goes and closes the door, and comes back.

We surely can't afford
Another scene like that we had just now;

Was ever anyone so caught before!
Damis did frighten me most terribly
On your account; you saw I did my best
To baffle his design, and calm his anger.
But I was so confused, I never thought
To contradict his story; still, thank Heaven,
Things turned out all the better, as it happened,
And now we're on an even safer footing.
The high esteem you're held in, laid the storm;
My husband can have no suspicion of you,
And even insists, to spite the scandal-mongers,
That we shall be together constantly;
So that is how, without the risk of blame,
I can be here locked up with you alone,
And can reveal to you my heart, perhaps
Only too ready to allow your passion.

TARTUFFE

Your words are somewhat hard to understand,
Madam; just now you used a different style.

ELMIRE

If that refusal has offended you,
How little do you know a woman's heart!
How ill you guess what it would have you know,
When it presents so feeble a defence!
Always, at first, our modesty resists
The tender feelings you inspire us with.
Whatever cause we find to justify
The love that masters us, we still must feel
Some little shame in owning it; and strive
To make as though we would not, when we would.
But from the very way we go about it
We let a lover know our heart surrenders,
The while our lips, for honour's sake, oppose
Our heart's desire, and in refusing promise.
I'm telling you my secret all too freely
And with too little heed to modesty.
But now that I've made bold to speak pray tell me.
Should I have tried to keep Damis from speaking,
Should I have heard the offer of your heart
So quietly, and suffered all your pleading,
And taken it just as I did remember
If such a declaration had not pleased me,
And, when I tried my utmost to persuade you
Not to accept the marriage that was talked of,
What should my earnestness have hinted to you
If not the interest that you've inspired,

And my chagrin, should such a match compel me
To share a heart I want all to myself?

TARTUFFE
'Tis, past a doubt, the height of happiness,
To hear such words from lips we dote upon;
Their honeyed sweetness pours through all my senses
Long draughts of suavity ineffable.
My heart employs its utmost zeal to please you,
And counts your love its one beatitude;
And yet that heart must beg that you allow it
To doubt a little its felicity.
I well might think these words an honest trick
To make me break off this approaching marriage;
And if I may express myself quite plainly,
I cannot trust these too enchanting words
Until the granting of some little favour
I sigh for, shall assure me of their truth
And build within my soul, on firm foundations,
A lasting faith in your sweet charity.

ELMIRE [Coughing to draw her **HUSBAND'S** attention]
What! Must you go so fast? and all at once
Exhaust the whole love of a woman's heart?
She does herself the violence to make
This dear confession of her love, and you
Are not yet satisfied, and will not be
Without the granting of her utmost favours?

TARTUFFE
The less a blessing is deserved, the less
We dare to hope for it; and words alone
Can ill assuage our love's desires. A fate
Too full of happiness, seems doubtful still;
We must enjoy it ere we can believe it.
And I, who know how little I deserve
Your goodness, doubt the fortunes of my daring;
So I shall trust to nothing, madam, till
You have convinced my love by something real.

ELMIRE
Ah! How your love enacts the tyrant's rôle,
And throws my mind into a strange confusion!
With what fierce sway it rules a conquered heart,
And violently will have its wishes granted!
What! Is there no escape from your pursuit?
No respite even? not a breathing space?
Nay, is it decent to be so exacting,

And so abuse by urgency the weakness
You may discover in a woman's heart?

TARTUFFE
But if my worship wins your gracious favour,
Then why refuse me some sure proof thereof?

ELMIRE
But how can I consent to what you wish,
Without offending Heaven you talk so much of?

TARTUFFE
If Heaven is all that stands now in my way,
I'll easily remove that little hindrance;
Your heart need not hold back for such a trifle.

ELMIRE
But they affright us so with Heaven's commands!

TARTUFFE
I can dispel these foolish fears, dear madam;
I know the art of pacifying scruples
Heaven forbids, 'tis true, some satisfactions;
But we find means to make things right with Heaven.
('Tis a scoundrel speaking.)
There is a science, madam, that instructs us
How to enlarge the limits of our conscience
According to our various occasions,
And rectify the evil of the deed
According to our purity of motive.
I'll duly teach you all these secrets, madam;
You only need to let yourself be guided.
Content my wishes, have no fear at all;
I answer for't, and take the sin upon me.

[**ELMIRE** coughs still louder.

Your cough is very bad.

ELMIRE
Yes, I'm in torture.

TARTUFFE
Would you accept this bit of licorice?

ELMIRE
The case is obstinate, I find; and all
The licorice in the world will do no good.

TARTUFFE
'Tis very trying.

ELMIRE
More than words can say.

TARTUFFE
In any case, your scruple's easily
Removed. With me you're sure of secrecy,
And there's no harm unless a thing is known.
The public scandal is what brings offence,
And secret sinning is not sin at all.

ELMIRE [After coughing again]
So then, I see I must resolve to yield;
I must consent to grant you everything,
And cannot hope to give full satisfaction
Or win full confidence, at lesser cost.
No doubt 'tis very hard to come to this;
'Tis quite against my will I go so far;
But since I must be forced to it, since nothing
That can be said suffices for belief,
Since more convincing proof is still demanded,
I must make up my mind to humour people.
If my consent give reason for offence,
So much the worse for him who forced me to it;
The fault can surely not be counted mine.

TARTUFFE
It need not, madam; and the thing itself ...

ELMIRE
Open the door, I pray you, and just see
Whether my husband's not there, in the hall.

TARTUFFE
Why take such care for him? Between ourselves,
He is a man to lead round by the nose.
He's capable of glorying in our meetings;
I've fooled him so, he'd see all, and deny it.

ELMIRE
No matter; go, I beg you, look about,
And carefully examine every corner.

SCENE VI

ORGON, ELMIRE

ORGON [Crawling out from under the table]
That is, I own, a man ... abominable!
I can't get over it; the whole thing floors me.

ELMIRE
What? You come out so soon? You cannot mean it!
Get back under the table; 'tis not time yet;
Wait till the end, to see, and make quite certain,
And don't believe a thing on mere conjecture.

ORGON
Nothing more wicked e'er came out of Hell.

ELMIRE
Dear me! Don't go and credit things too lightly.
No, let yourself be thoroughly convinced;
Don't yield too soon, for fear you'll be mistaken.

[As **TARTUFFE** enters, she makes her **HUSBAND** stand behind her.

SCENE VII

TARTUFFE, ELMIRE, ORGON

TARTUFFE [Not seeing **ORGON**]
All things conspire toward my satisfaction,
Madam, I've searched the whole apartment through.
There's no one here; and now my ravished soul ...

ORGON [Stopping him]
Softly! You are too eager in your amours;
You needn't be so passionate. Ah ha!
My holy man! You want to put it on me!
How is your soul abandoned to temptation!
Marry my daughter, eh? and want my wife, too?
I doubted long enough if this was earnest,
Expecting all the time the tone would change;
But now the proof's been carried far enough;
I'm satisfied, and ask no more, for my part.

ELMIRE [To **TARTUFFE**]
'Twas quite against my character to play

This part; but I was forced to treat you so.

TARTUFFE
What? You believe ...

ORGON
Come, now, no protestations.
Get out from here, and make no fuss about it.

TARTUFFE
But my intent ...

ORGON
That talk is out of season.
You leave my house this instant.

TARTUFFE
You're the one
To leave it, you who play the master here!
This house belongs to me, I'll have you know,
And show you plainly it's no use to turn
To these low tricks, to pick a quarrel with me,
And that you can't insult me at your pleasure,
For I have wherewith to confound your lies,
Avenge offended Heaven, and compel
Those to repent who talk to me of leaving.

SCENE VIII

ELMIRE, ORGON

ELMIRE
What sort of speech is this? What can it mean?

ORGON
My faith, I'm dazed. This is no laughing matter.

ELMIRE
What?

ORGON
From his words I see my great mistake;
The deed of gift is one thing troubles me.

ELMIRE
The deed of gift ...

ORGON
Yes, that is past recall.
But I've another thing to make me anxious.

ELMIRE
What's that?

ORGON
You shall know all. Let's see at once
Whether a certain box is still upstairs.

ACT V

SCENE I

ORGON, CLEANTE.

CLEANTE
Whither away so fast?

ORGON
How should I know?

CLEANTE
Methinks we should begin by taking counsel
To see what can be done to meet the case.

ORGON
I'm all worked up about that wretched box.
More than all else it drives me to despair.

CLEANTE
That box must hide some mighty mystery?

ORGON
Argas, my friend who is in trouble, brought it
Himself, most secretly, and left it with me.
He chose me, in his exile, for this trust;
And on these documents, from what he said,
I judge his life and property depend.

CLEANTE
How could you trust them to another's hands?

ORGON

By reason of a conscientious scruple.
I went straight to my traitor, to confide
In him; his sophistry made me believe
That I must give the box to him to keep,
So that, in case of search, I might deny
My having it at all, and still, by favour
Of this evasion, keep my conscience clear
Even in taking oath against the truth.

CLEANTE
Your case is bad, so far as I can see;
This deed of gift, this trusting of the secret
To him, were both to state my frank opinion
Steps that you took too lightly; he can lead you
To any length, with these for hostages;
And since he holds you at such disadvantage,
You'd be still more imprudent, to provoke him;
So you must go some gentler way about.

ORGON
What! Can a soul so base, a heart so false,
Hide neath the semblance of such touching fervour?
I took him in, a vagabond, a beggar! ...
'Tis too much! No more pious folk for me!
I shall abhor them utterly forever,
And henceforth treat them worse than any devil.

CLEANTE
So! There you go again, quite off the handle!
In nothing do you keep an even temper.
You never know what reason is, but always
Jump first to one extreme, and then the other.
You see your error, and you recognise
That you've been cozened by a feigned zeal;
But to make up for't, in the name of reason,
Why should you plunge into a worse mistake,
And find no difference in character
Between a worthless scamp, and all good people?
What! Just because a rascal boldly duped you
With pompous show of false austerity,
Must you needs have it everybody's like him,
And no one's truly pious nowadays?
Leave such conclusions to mere infidels;
Distinguish virtue from its counterfeit,
Don't give esteem too quickly, at a venture,
But try to keep, in this, the golden mean.
If you can help it, don't uphold imposture;
But do not rail at true devoutness, either;

And if you must fall into one extreme,
Then rather err again the other way.

SCENE II

DAMIS, ORGON, CLEANTE.

DAMIS
What! father, can the scoundrel threaten you,
Forget the many benefits received,
And in his base abominable pride
Make of your very favours arms against you?

ORGON
Too true, my son. It tortures me to think on't.

DAMIS
Let me alone, I'll chop his ears off for him.
We must deal roundly with his insolence;
'Tis I must free you from him at a blow;
'Tis I, to set things right, must strike him down.

CLEANTE
Spoke like a true young man. Now just calm down,
And moderate your towering tantrums, will you?
We live in such an age, with such a king,
That violence can not advance our cause.

SCENE III

Madame PERNELLE, ORGON, ELMIRE, CLEANTE, MARIANE, DAMIS, DORINE.

Madame PERNELLE
What's this? I hear of fearful mysteries!

ORGON
Strange things indeed, for my own eyes to witness;
You see how I'm requited for my kindness,
I zealously receive a wretched beggar,
I lodge him, entertain him like my brother,
Load him with benefactions every day,
Give him my daughter, give him all my fortune:
And he meanwhile, the villain, rascal, wretch,
Tries with black treason to suborn my wife,

And not content with such a foul design,
He dares to menace me with my own favours,
And would make use of those advantages
Which my too foolish kindness armed him with,
To ruin me, to take my fortune from me,
And leave me in the state I saved him from.

DORINE
Poor man!

Madame PERNELLE
My son, I cannot possibly
Believe he could intend so black a deed.

ORGON
What?

Madame PERNELLE
Worthy men are still the sport of envy.

ORGON
Mother, what do you mean by such a speech?

Madame PERNELLE
There are strange goings-on about your house,
And everybody knows your people hate him.

ORGON
What's that to do with what I tell you now?

Madame PERNELLE
I always said, my son, when you were little:
That virtue here below is hated ever;
The envious may die, but envy never.

ORGON
What's that fine speech to do with present facts?

Madame PERNELLE
Be sure, they've forged a hundred silly lies ...

ORGON
I've told you once, I saw it all myself.

Madame PERNELLE
For slanderers abound in calumnies ...

ORGON

Mother, you'd make me damn my soul. I tell you
I saw with my own eyes his shamelessness.

Madame PERNELLE
Their tongues for spitting venom never lack,
There's nothing here below they'll not attack.

ORGON
Your speech has not a single grain of sense.
I saw it, harkee, saw it, with these eyes
I saw d'ye know what saw means? must I say it
A hundred times, and din it in your ears?

Madame PERNELLE
My dear, appearances are oft deceiving,
And seeing shouldn't always be believing.

ORGON
I'll go mad.

Madame PERNELLE
False suspicions may delude,
And good to evil oft is misconstrued.

ORGON
Must I construe as Christian charity
The wish to kiss my wife!

Madame PERNELLE
You must, at least,
Have just foundation for accusing people,
And wait until you see a thing for sure.

ORGON
The devil! How could I see any surer?
Should I have waited till, before my eyes,
He ... No, you'll make me say things quite improper.

Madame PERNELLE
In short, 'tis known too pure a zeal inflames him;
And so, I cannot possibly conceive
That he should try to do what's charged against him.

ORGON
If you were not my mother, I should say
Such things! ... I know not what, I'm so enraged!

DORINE [To **ORGON**]

Fortune has paid you fair, to be so doubted;
You flouted our report, now yours is flouted.

CLEANTE
We're wasting time here in the merest trifling,
Which we should rather use in taking measures
To guard ourselves against the scoundrel's threats.

DAMIS
You think his impudence could go far?

ELMIRE
For one, I can't believe it possible;
Why, his ingratitude would be too patent.

CLEANTE
Don't trust to that; he'll find abundant warrant
To give good colour to his acts against you;
And for less cause than this, a strong cabal
Can make one's life a labyrinth of troubles.
I tell you once again: armed as he is
You never should have pushed him quite so far.

ORGON
True; yet what could I do? The rascal's pride
Made me lose all control of my resentment.

CLEANTE
I wish with all my heart that some pretence
Of peace could be patched up between you two

ELMIRE
If I had known what weapons he was armed with,
I never should have raised such an alarm,
And my ...

ORGON [To **DORINE**, seeing **MR. LOYAL** come in]
Who's coming now? Go quick, find out.
I'm in a fine state to receive a visit!

SCENE IV

ORGON, Madame PERNELLE, ELMIRE, MARIANE, CLEANTE, DAMIS, DORINE, MR. LOYAL.

MR. LOYAL [To **DORINE**, at the back of the stage]
Good day, good sister. Pray you, let me see

The master of the house.

DORINE
He's occupied;
I think he can see nobody at present.

MR. LOYAL
I'm not by way of being unwelcome here.
My coming can, I think, nowise displease him;
My errand will be found to his advantage.

DORINE
Your name, then?

MR. LOYAL
Tell him simply that his friend
Mr. Tartuffe has sent me, for his goods ...

DORINE [To **ORGON**]
It is a man who comes, with civil manners,
Sent by Tartuffe, he says, upon an errand
That you'll be pleased with.

CLEANTE [To **ORGON**]
Surely you must see him,
And find out who he is, and what he wants.

ORGON [To **CLEANTE**]
Perhaps he's come to make it up between us:
How shall I treat him?

CLEANTE
You must not get angry;
And if he talks of reconciliation
Accept it.

MR. LOYAL [To **ORGON**]
Sir, good-day. And Heaven send
Harm to your enemies, favour to you.

ORGON [Aside to **CLEANTE**]
This mild beginning suits with my conjectures
And promises some compromise already.

MR. LOYAL
All of your house has long been dear to me;
I had the honour, sir, to serve your father.

ORGON
Sir, I am much ashamed, and ask your pardon
For not recalling now your face or name.

MR. LOYAL
My name is Loyal. I'm from Normandy.
My office is court-bailiff, in despite
Of envy; and for forty years, thank Heaven,
It's been my fortune to perform that office
With honour. So I've come, sir, by your leave
To render service of a certain writ ...

ORGON
What, you are here to ...

MR. LOYAL
Pray, sir, don't be angry.
'Tis nothing, sir, but just a little summons:
Order to vacate, you and yours, this house,
Move out your furniture, make room for others,
And that without delay or putting off,
As needs must be ...

ORGON
I? Leave this house?

MR. LOYAL
Yes, please, sir
The house is now, as you well know, of course,
Mr. Tartuffe's. And he, beyond dispute,
Of all your goods is henceforth lord and master
By virtue of a contract here attached,
Drawn in due form, and unassailable.

DAMIS [To **MR. LOYAL**]
Your insolence is monstrous, and astounding!

MR. LOYAL [To **DAMIS**]
I have no business, sir, that touches you;
[Pointing to **ORGON**]
This is the gentleman. He's fair and courteous,
And knows too well a gentleman's behaviour
To wish in any wise to question justice.

ORGON
But ...

MR. LOYAL

Sir, I know you would not for a million
Wish to rebel; like a good citizen
You'll let me put in force the court's decree.

DAMIS
Your long black gown may well, before you know it,
Mister Court-bailiff, get a thorough beating.

MR. LOYAL [To **ORGON**]
Sir, make your son be silent or withdraw.
I should be loath to have to set things down,
And see your names inscribed in my report.

DORINE [Aside]
This Mr. Loyal's looks are most disloyal.

MR. LOYAL
I have much feeling for respectable
And honest folk like you, sir, and consented
To serve these papers, only to oblige you,
And thus prevent the choice of any other
Who, less possessed of zeal for you than I am
Might order matters in less gentle fashion.

ORGON
And how could one do worse than order people
Out of their house?

MR. LOYAL
Why, we allow you time;
And even will suspend until to-morrow
The execution of the order, sir.
I'll merely, without scandal, quietly,
Come here and spend the night, with half a score
Of officers; and just for form's sake, please,
You'll bring your keys to me, before retiring.
I will take care not to disturb your rest,
And see there's no unseemly conduct here.
But by to-morrow, and at early morning,
You must make haste to move your least belongings;
My men will help you I have chosen strong ones
To serve you, sir, in clearing out the house.
No one could act more generously, I fancy,
And, since I'm treating you with great indulgence,
I beg you'll do as well by me, and see
I'm not disturbed in my discharge of duty.

ORGON

I'd give this very minute, and not grudge it,
The hundred best gold louis I have left,
If I could just indulge myself, and land
My fist, for one good square one, on his snout.

CLEANTE [Aside to **ORGON**]
Careful! don't make things worse.

DAMIS
Such insolence!
I hardly can restrain myself. My hands
Are itching to be at him.

DORINE
By my faith,
With such a fine broad back, good Mr. Loyal,
A little beating would become you well.

MR. LOYAL
My girl, such infamous words are actionable.
And warrants can be issued against women.

CLEANTE [To **MR. LOYAL**]
Enough of this discussion, sir; have done.
Give us the paper, and then leave us, pray.

MR. LOYAL
Then au revoir . Heaven keep you from disaster!

ORGON
May Heaven confound you both, you and your master!

SCENE V

ORGON, Madame PERNELLE, ELMIRE, CLEANTE, MARIANE, DAMIS, DORINE.

ORGON
Well, mother, am I right or am I not?
This writ may help you now to judge the matter.
Or don't you see his treason even yet?

Madame PERNELLE
I'm all amazed, befuddled, and beflustered!

DORINE [To **ORGON**]
You are quite wrong, you have no right to blame him;

This action only proves his good intentions.
Love for his neighbour makes his virtue perfect;
And knowing money is a root of evil,
In Christian charity, he'd take away
Whatever things may hinder your salvation.

ORGON
Be still. You always need to have that told you.

CLEANTE [To **ORGON**]
Come, let us see what course you are to follow.

ELMIRE
Go and expose his bold ingratitude.
Such action must invalidate the contract;
His perfidy must now appear too black
To bring him the success that he expects.

SCENE VI

VALÈRE, ORGON, Madame PERNELLE, ELMIRE, CLEANTE, MARIANE, DAMIS, DORINE.

VALÈRE
'Tis with regret, sir, that I bring bad news;
But urgent danger forces me to do so.
A close and intimate friend of mine, who knows
The interest I take in what concerns you,
Has gone so far, for my sake, as to break
The secrecy that's due to state affairs,
And sent me word but now, that leaves you only
The one expedient of sudden flight.
The villain who so long imposed upon you,
Found means, an hour ago, to see the prince,
And to accuse you (among other things)
By putting in his hands the private strong-box
Of a state-criminal, whose guilty secret,
You, failing in your duty as a subject,
(He says) have kept. I know no more of it
Save that a warrant's drawn against you, sir,
And for the greater surety, that same rascal
Comes with the officer who must arrest you.

CLEANTE
His rights are armed; and this is how the scoundrel
Seeks to secure the property he claims.

ORGON
Man is a wicked animal, I'll own it!

VALÈRE
The least delay may still be fatal, sir.
I have my carriage, and a thousand louis,
Provided for your journey, at the door.
Let's lose no time; the bolt is swift to strike,
And such as only flight can save you from.
I'll be your guide to seek a place of safety,
And stay with you until you reach it, sir.

ORGON
How much I owe to your obliging care!
Another time must serve to thank you fitly;
And I pray Heaven to grant me so much favour
That I may some day recompense your service.
Good-bye; see to it, all of you ...

CLEANTE
Come hurry;
We'll see to everything that's needful, brother.

SCENE VII

TARTUFFE, an **OFFICER**, Madame **PERNELLE**, **ORGON**, **ELMIRE**, **CLEANTE**, **MARIANE**, **VALÈRE**, **DAMIS**,
DORINE.

TARTUFFE [Stopping **ORGON**]
Softly, sir, softly; do not run so fast;
You haven't far to go to find your lodging;
By order of the prince, we here arrest you.

ORGON
Traitor! You saved this worst stroke for the last;
This crowns your perfidies, and ruins me.

TARTUFFE
I shall not be embittered by your insults,
For Heaven has taught me to endure all things.

CLEANTE
Your moderation, I must own, is great.

DAMIS
How shamelessly the wretch makes bold with Heaven!

TARTUFFE
Your ravings cannot move me; all my thought
Is but to do my duty.

MARIANE
You must claim
Great glory from this honourable act.

TARTUFFE
The act cannot be aught but honourable,
Coming from that high power which sends me here.

ORGON
Ungrateful wretch, do you forget 'twas I
That rescued you from utter misery?

TARTUFFE
I've not forgot some help you may have given;
But my first duty now is toward my prince.
The higher power of that most sacred claim
Must stifle in my heart all gratitude;
And to such puissant ties I'd sacrifice
My friend, my wife, my kindred, and myself.

ELMIRE
The hypocrite!

DORINE
How well he knows the trick
Of cloaking him with what we most revere!

CLEANTE
But if the motive that you make parade of
Is perfect as you say, why should it wait
To show itself, until the day he caught you
Soliciting his wife? How happens it
You have not thought to go inform against him
Until his honour forces him to drive you
Out of his house? And though I need not mention
That he'd just given you his whole estate,
Still, if you meant to treat him now as guilty,
How could you then consent to take his gift?

TARTUFFE [To the **OFFICER**]
Pray, sir, deliver me from all this clamour;
Be good enough to carry out your order.

THE OFFICER
Yes, I've too long delayed its execution;
'Tis very fitting you should urge me to it;
So therefore, you must follow me at once
To prison, where you'll find your lodging ready.

TARTUFFE
Who? I, sir?

THE OFFICER
You.

TARTUFFE
By why to prison?

THE OFFICER
You
Are not the one to whom I owe account.
You, sir
[To **ORGON**]
—recover from your hot alarm.
Our prince is not a friend to double dealing,
His eyes can read men's inmost hearts, and all
The art of hypocrites cannot deceive him.
His sharp discernment sees things clear and true;
His mind cannot too easily be swayed,
For reason always holds the balance even.
He honours and exalts true piety,
But knows the false, and views it with disgust.
This fellow was by no means apt to fool him,
Far subtler snares have failed against his wisdom,
And his quick insight pierced immediately
The hidden baseness of this tortuous heart.
Accusing you, the knave betrayed himself,
And by true recompense of Heaven's justice
He stood revealed before our monarch's eyes
A scoundrel known before by other names,
Whose horrid crimes, detailed at length, might fill
A long-drawn history of many volumes.
Our monarch to resolve you in a word
Detesting his ingratitude and baseness,
Added this horror to his other crimes,
And sent me hither under his direction
To see his insolence out-top itself,
And force him then to give you satisfaction.
Your papers, which the traitor says are his,
I am to take from him, and give you back;
The deed of gift transferring your estate

Our monarch's sovereign will makes null and void;
And for the secret personal offence
Your friend involved you in, he pardons you:
Thus he rewards your recent zeal, displayed
In helping to maintain his rights, and shows
How well his heart, when it is least expected,
Knows how to recompense a noble deed,
And will not let true merit miss its due,
Remembering always rather good than evil.

DORINE
Now Heaven be praised!

Madame PERNELLE
At last I breathe again.

ELMIRE
A happy outcome!

MARIANE
Who'd have dared to hope it?

ORGON [To **TARTUFFE**, who is being led by the **OFFICER**]
There traitor! Now you're ...

SCENE VIII

Madame PERNELLE, ORGON, ELMIRE, MARIANE, CLEANTE, VALÈRE, DAMIS, DORINE.

CLEANTE
Brother, hold! and don't
Descend to such indignities, I beg you.
Leave the poor wretch to his unhappy fate,
And let remorse oppress him, but not you.
Hope rather that his heart may now return
To virtue, hate his vice, reform his ways,
And win the pardon of our glorious prince;
While you must straightway go, and on your knees
Repay with thanks his noble generous kindness.

ORGON
Well said! We'll go, and at his feet kneel down,
With joy to thank him for his goodness shown;
And this first duty done, with honours due,
We'll then attend upon another, too.
With wedded happiness reward Valère,

And crown a lover noble and sincere.

Molière – A Short Biography

Jean-Baptiste Poquelin is better known to us by his stage name of Molière. He was born in Paris, to a prosperous well-to-do family, the son of Jean Poquelin and Marie Cressé, on 15th January 1622.

It is said that a maid, seeing him for the first time shrieked, "Le nez!", a reference to the infant's large nose. The name stuck as a family nickname from that time. At ten his mother died and his relationship with his father seems to have been lukewarm at best.

It is probable that his education started with studies in a Parisian elementary school. This was followed with his enrolment in the prestigious Jesuit Collège de Clermont, where he completed his studies in a strict academic environment but also first sampled life on the stage.

In 1631, his father purchased from the court of Louis XIII the posts of "valet de chambre ordinaire et tapissier du Roi" ("valet of the King's chamber and keeper of carpets and upholstery").

Molière assumed his father's posts in 1641. The benefits included only three months' work per annum for which he was paid 300 livres and also provided a number of lucrative contracts.

To increase the spectrum of his skills Molière also studied as a provincial lawyer around 1642, probably in Orléans, but it is not recorded if he ever qualified. Up to this date he had followed his father's plans for a career and they had served him well; he seemed destined for a career in office.

However, in June 1643, when he was 21, Molière abandoned this path for his first love; a career on the stage. He partnered with the actress Madeleine Béjart, to found the Illustre Théâtre at a cost of 630 livres.

Unfortunately, despite their enthusiasm, effort and ambition the troupe went bankrupt in 1645. Molière, now in charge, due to both his acting prowess and his legal training, had run up debts, mainly for the rent of the theatre, of 2000 livres. Molière was thrown into prison. Historians differ as to who paid the debts but after a 24-hour stint in jail Molière returned to the acting circuit.

It was at this time that he began to use the pseudonym Molière. It may also have been to spare his father the shame of having an actor in the family; a lowly profession for his status in society.

Molière and Madeleine now began with a new group of actors and spent the next dozen years touring the provincial circuit. The company slowly gained in success. Molière was also writing much of what they acted. Sadly only a few plays survive from this period among them 'The Bungler' and 'The Doctor in Love'. They represent though a distinct move away from the Italian improvisational Commedia dell'arte and highlight his use of mockery.

Armand, Prince of Conti, the governor of Languedoc, now also became his patron in return the company was named after him. Sadly for Molière the friendship later ended when Conti, having contracted syphilis from a courtesan, turned towards religion and joined Molière's enemies in the Parti des Dévots and the Compagnie de Saint Sacrement.

Molière's' journey back to the sacred land of Parisian theatres was slow. However by 1658 he performed in front of the King at the Louvre (then a theatre for hire) in Corneille's tragedy 'Nicomède' and in the farce 'Le Docteur Amoureux' (The Doctor in Love) with some success. He was awarded the title of Troupe de Monsieur (Monsieur being the honorific for the king's brother Philippe I, Duke of Orléans). With the help of Monsieur, his company was allowed to share the theatre in the large hall of the Petit-Bourbon with the famous Italian Commedia dell'arte company of Tiberio Fiorillo. The companies performed in the theatre on alternate nights.

The premiere of Molière's 'Les Précieuses Ridicules' (The Affected Young Ladies) took place at the Petit-Bourbon on 18th November 1659. It was the first of Molière's many attempts to satirize certain societal mannerisms and affectations then common in France. It won Molière the attention and the criticism of many, but alas not a large audience. He then asked Fiorillo to teach him the techniques of Commedia dell'arte. His 1660 play 'Sganarelle, ou Le Cocu imaginaire' (The Imaginary Cuckold) seems to be a tribute both to Commedia dell'arte and to his teacher.

Despite his own preference for tragedy, Molière became famous for these farces, which were generally in one act and performed after the tragedy. Some of these farces were only partly written and performed in the style of Commedia dell'arte with improvisation over a sketched out plot. He also wrote two comedies in verse, but these were less successful.

In 1660 the Petit-Bourbon was demolished to make way for the expansion of the Louvre. Molière's company decamped to the abandoned theatre in the Palais-Royal which was in the process of being refurbished. The company opened there on 20th January 1661. In order to please his patron, Monsieur, who was so enthralled with the arts that he was soon excluded from state affairs, Molière wrote and played 'Dom Garcie de Navarre ou Le Prince jaloux' (The Jealous Prince, 4th February 1661), a heroic comedy derived from a work of Cicognini's. Two other comedies of the same year were the successful 'L'École des maris' (The School for Husbands) and 'Les Fâcheux', (The Mad also known as The Bores) subtitled Comédie faite pour les divertissements du Roi (a comedy for the King's amusements) as it was performed during a series of parties that Nicolas Fouquet gave in honor of the king. These entertainments led to the arrest of Fouquet for wasting public money. He was sentenced to life imprisonment.

In parallel with 'Les Fâcheux', Molière introduced the comédies-ballets. These ballets were a transitional form of dance performance between the court ballets of Louis XIV and the art of professional theatre which was developing rapidly with the use of the proscenium stage. The comédies-ballets developed by chance when Molière was enlisted to mount both a play and a ballet in the honor of Louis XIV and found that he did not have a large enough cast to meet the needs of both. Cleverly Molière decided to combine the ballet and the play to achieve his goals. The gamble paid off handsomely. Molière was asked to produce twelve more comédies-ballets before his death. During these Molière collaborated with Pierre Beauchamp. Beauchamp codified the five balletic positions of the feet and arms and was partly responsible for the creation of the Beauchamp-Feuillet dance notation. He also collaborated with Jean-Baptiste Lully, a dancer, choreographer, and composer, whose reign at the Paris Opéra ran for fifteen years. Under Molière's command, ballet and opera became professional arts unto themselves. The comédies-ballets closely integrated dance with music and the action of the play and the style of continuity distinctly separated these performances from the court ballets of the time; additionally, the comédies-ballets demanded that both the dancers and the actors play an important role in advancing the story. Intriguingly Louis XIV played the part of an Egyptian in 'Le Mariage forcé' (1664) and also appeared as Neptune and Apollo in his retirement performance of 'Les Amants magnifiques' (1670).

On 20th February 1662 Molière married Armande Béjart, whom he believed to be the sister of Madeleine. The same year he premiered 'L'École des Femmes' (The School for Wives), widely regarded as a masterpiece. It poked fun at the limited education given to daughters of rich families and reflected on Molière's own marriage. It attracted a lot of outraged criticism and ignited the protest called the "Quarrel of L'École des femmes". Molière responded with two works: 'La Critique de "L'École des femmes"', in which he imagined the audience of the previous work attending it. It mocks them by presenting them at dinner after watching the play; it addresses all the criticism raised about the piece by presenting the critics' arguments and then dismissing them. This was the so-called Guerre comique (War of Comedy), in which the opposite side was taken by writers like Donneau de Visé, Edmé Boursault, and Montfleury.

But more serious opposition was brewing, focusing on Molière's politics and his personal life. Some in French high society protested against Molière's excessive realism and irreverence, which were causing some embarrassment. Despite this the King expressed support for him. Molière was granted a pension and the King agreed to be the godfather of Molière's first son.

Molière's friendship with Jean-Baptiste Lully influenced him towards writing his 'Le Mariage forcé' and 'La Princesse d'Élide', written for royal divertissements at the Palace of Versailles.

'Tartuffe, ou L'Imposteur' was also performed at Versailles, in 1664, and created the greatest scandal of Molière's artistic career. Its depiction of the hypocrisy of the dominant classes was taken as an outrage and violently contested. It also aroused the wrath of the Jansenists (a Catholic theological movement, that emphasized original sin, human depravity, the necessity of divine grace, and predestination). The play was banned.

Molière was always careful not to attack the monarchy in any way. He had won a position as one of the king's favourites and enjoyed his protection from the attacks of the court. When the King suggested that Molière suspend performances of 'Tartuffe', Molière complied and quickly wrote 'Dom Juan ou le Festin de Pierre' (Don Juan, or, The Stone Banquet) to replace it. The story is of an atheist who becomes a religious hypocrite and is punished by God. But this too fell foul and was quickly suspended. The King, still keen to protect Molière became the new official sponsor of Molière's troupe.

With music by Lully, Molière presented 'Love Doctor or Medical Love'. The work was given "par ordre du Roi" (by order of the King) and was received much more warmly than its predecessors.

In 1666, 'Le Misanthrope' was produced. Molière's masterpiece. Although brimming with moral content it was little appreciated at the time and a commercial flop, forcing Molière to immediately write 'The Doctor Despite Himself', a satire against the official sciences. This was a success despite a moral treatise by the Prince of Conti, criticizing the theater in general and Molière in particular.

After the Mélicerte and the Pastorale comique, he tried again to perform a revised 'Tartuffe' in 1667, this time with the name of Panulphe or L'Imposteur. As soon as the King left Paris for a tour, the play was banned. The King finally imposed respect for 'Tartuffe' some years later, when he gained more power over the clergy.

Molière, now ill, wrote at a slower pace. 'Le Sicilien ou L'Amour peintre' (The Sicilian, or Love the Painter) was written for festivities at the castle of Saint-Germain-en-Laye, and was followed in 1668 by 'Amphitryon'.

'George Dandin, ou Le mari confondu' (The Confounded Husband) was little appreciated, but success returned with 'L'Avare' (The Miser), now very well known.

With Lully he again used music for 'Monsieur de Pourceaugnac', for 'Les Amants magnifiques' (The Magnificent Lovers), and finally for 'Le Bourgeois gentilhomme' (The Middle-Class Gentleman), another of his masterpieces. The collaboration with Lully ended with a tragédie et ballet, 'Psyché', written in collaboration with Pierre Corneille and Philippe Quinault.

In 1672, Madeleine Béjart died. It was a heavy blow to Molière who was already in declining health himself. However, he continued to write and his plays were eagerly awaited and performed. 'Les Fourberies de Scapin' (The Impostures of Scapin), a farce and a comedy in five acts was successful. The following play, 'La Comtesse d'Escarbagnas' (The Countess of Escarbagnas), is thought of as a lesser works.

'Les Femmes savantes' (The Learned Ladies) of 1672 is accepted as another masterpieces. It was born from the termination of the legal use of music in theater, (Lully had patented the opera in France and taken the best singers for his own works), so Molière returned to his traditional genre. It was a great success.

Molière suffered from pulmonary tuberculosis. One of the most famous moments in Molière's life was his last: he collapsed on stage in a fit of coughing and haemorrhaging while performing in the last play he'd written, in which, ironically, he was playing the hypochondriac Argan, in 'The Imaginary Invalid'.

Molière insisted on completing his performance.

Afterwards he collapsed again with another, larger haemorrhage and was taken home. Priests were sent for to administer the last rites. Two priests refused to visit. A third arrived too late. On 17th February 1673, Jean-Baptiste Poquelin, forever to be known as Molière, was pronounced dead in Paris. He was 51.

Under French law at the time, actors were forbidden to be buried in sacred ground. Molière's widow asked the King if Molière could be granted a normal funeral at night. The King agreed.

In his life Molière divided opinion. He was adored by the court and Parisians but loathed and reviled by moralists and the Catholic Church.

In 1792 his remains were brought to the museum of French monuments. In 1817 they were transferred to Père Lachaise Cemetery in Paris, close to those of La Fontaine.

In his 14 years in Paris, Molière singlehandedly wrote 31 of the 85 plays performed on his stage. His immensely popular legacy includes comedies, farces, tragicomedies and comédie-ballets.

Molière – A Concise Bibliography

Le Médecin Volant (1645)—The Flying Doctor
La Jalousie du Barbouillé (1650)—The Jealousy of le Barbouillé
L'Étourdi, ou le Contre-Temps(1653)—The Scatterbrain or The Bungler
L'Étourdi ou les Contretemps (1655)—The Blunderer, or, the Counterplots
Le Dépit Amoureux (16 December 1656)—The Love-Tiff
Le Docteur Amoureux (1658), 1st play performed by Molière's troupe (now lost)—The Doctor in Love
Les Précieuses Ridicules (1659)—The Affected Young Ladies
Sganarelle ou Le Cocu Imaginaire (1660)— Sganarelle or, The Self-Deceived Husband aka The Imaginary Cuckold
Dom Garcie de Navarre ou Le Prince Jaloux (1661)—Don Garcia of Navarre or the Jealous Prince
L'École des Maris (1661)—The School for Husbands
Les Fâcheux (17 August 1661)—The Mad aka The Bores
L'École des Femmes (1662; adapted into The Amorous Flea, 1964)—The School for Wives
La Jalousie du Gros-René (1663)—The Jealousy of Gros-René
La Critique de l'école des Femmes (1663)—Critique of the School for Wives
L'Impromptu de Versailles (1663)—The Versailles Impromptu
Le Mariage Forcé (1664)—The Forced Marriage
Gros-René, Petit Enfant (1664; now lost)—Gros-René, Small Child
La Princesse d'Élide (1664)—The Princess of Elid
Tartuffe ou L'Imposteur (1664)—Tartuffe, or, the Impostor
Dom Juan ou Le Festin de Pierre (1665)—Don Juan, or, The Stone Banquet (aka The Stone Guest, The Feast with the Statue)
L'Amour médecin (1665)—Love Is the Doctor aka Medical Love
Le Misanthrope ou L'Atrabilaire Amoureux (1666)—The Misanthrope, or, the Cantankerous Lover
Le Médecin Malgré Lui (1666)—The Physican in Spite of Himself aka A Doctor Despite Himself
Mélicerte (1666)
Pastorale Comique (1667)—Comic Pastoral
Le Sicilien ou L'Amour Peintre (1667)—The Sicilian, or Love the Painter
Amphitryon (1668)
George Dandin ou Le Mari Confondu (1668)—George Dandin, or, the Abashed Husband
L'Avare ou L'École du Mensonge (1668)—The Miser, or, the School for Lies
Monsieur de Pourceaugnac (1669)
Les Amants Magnifiques (1670)—The Magnificent Lovers
Le Bourgeois Gentilhomme (1670)—The Middle-Class Gentleman aka The Shopkeeper Turned Gentleman
Psyché (1671)—Psyche
Les Fourberies de Scapin (1671)—The Impostures of Scapin
La Comtesse d'Escarbagnas (1671)—The Countess of Escarbagnas
Les Femmes Savantes (1672)—The Learned Ladies aka The Learned Women
Le Malade Imaginaire (1673)—The Imaginary Invalid

Made in the USA
Middletown, DE
20 January 2024

48228601R00049